Ellis Island

Immigration's Shining Center

These newcomers bustling eagerly into Ellis Island c.1907 typified immigrants adhering to restrictions that they could only bring into the United States what they could carry—or wear. Thus women donned extra petticoats, skirts, sweaters, and even long coats to add to their possessions, even if the extra garments gave them an appearance of obesity.

THE MAKING OF AMERICA

Ellis Island

Immigration's Shining Center

JOHN T. CUNNINGHAM

ISBN 0-7385-2428-X

Published by Arcadia Publishing,
an imprint of Tempus Publishing, Inc.
Charleston SC, Chicago, Portsmouth NH, San Francisco

Printed in Great Britain.

Library of Congress Catalog Card Number: 2003110225

For all general information contact Arcadia Publishing at:
Telephone 843-853-2070
Fax 843-853-0044
E-Mail sales@arcadiapublishing.com
For customer service and orders:
Toll-Free 1-888-313-2665

Visit us on the Internet at http://www.arcadiapublishing.com

CONTENTS

6 Preface

11 From the Beginning: Immigrants All

21 A Nation Built on Immigrant Backs

30 The Castle of Dreams

41 "Give Me Your Tired, Your Poor"

48 Invitations to the Land of Gold

56 "It was Not a Desirable Place"

97 Island of Thieves

101 Goodbye to the Homeland

107 Down to the Very Bottom

117 The World's Most Awesome Island

128 "Committing a Gross Injustice"

133 The Tough Road to Americanization

141 Closing the Golden Door

147 Resurrecting a National Shrine

151 Appendix: Immigrants of Consequence

155 Bibliography

157 Index

PREFACE

When an early morning fog enshrouds New York harbor and the now vacated Central of New Jersey Railroad train shed on the Jersey City waterfront, an eerie feeling of oneness with immigrants of a century ago pervades the harbor. Directly east, the New York City skyline looms through the swirling mist. Slightly to the southeast is fog-enshrouded Ellis Island, America's symbol of immigration, and just beyond, the Statue of Liberty's torch gleams through occasional breaks in the rising haze.

Those three areas—the unused railroad station, Ellis Island, and the Statue of Liberty—encompass much of the vibrant, never-ending saga of newcomers striving to achieve a better life in the land called America.

Immigration is America's basic story, the source of the nation's strength and its uniqueness. No other nation in the world ever was founded on the principle that people of many lands can coexist and, indeed, thrive on the intermingled traits and customs brought here from more than a hundred foreign soils. Every American is descended from immigrants, even the so-called Native Americans—whose ancestors came from Asia and whose trek to what is now the United States took thousands of years and dozens of generations.

Ellis Island was the primary magnet in the greatest migration in human history, between 1892 and World War I. Day after day in that period, week after week, and month after month, ships anchored in the New York harbor, awaiting word that they could disembark the passengers who had ridden to America in steerage—that lowest portion of a ship where the steering mechanism could be seen and where normal life disappeared in the vapors, odors, and cruelties of the hold.

More than 15 million people passed through Ellis Island in its heyday between 1895 and 1916, most of them from southern and eastern Europe. They were called the "new immigrants" by a nation that from earliest colonial times had welcomed mainly Anglo-Saxons from northern Europe. The "new" immigrants—the Ellis Island immigrants—helped to transform the old nation and build a new society.

Preface

Except for the millions of Africans brutally kidnapped and shipped to America as slaves, all immigrants to America left their homes because they hoped, and believed, that the United States offered the world's best chance for freedom and opportunity.

While this book is fundamentally the Ellis Island story, it is by necessity also the broader story of a great nation explored by, colonized by, and constantly changed by persons who either came directly from abroad or were descended from those pioneers.

No matter how big, how magnificent, how sad, how moving the island's story is, it is in reality only one facet of the fascinating ability of a nation to absorb and reabsorb differing people—and often, in the process, forgetting that they too are descended from immigrants—brave, resourceful, stubborn, daring people.

Ferries leave Liberty Park in New Jersey or The Battery in Manhattan on regular schedules, stopping at both the island and the Statue of Liberty park. As these modern vessels approach Ellis Island, it doesn't take a fervent romantic to get a nostalgic, if fleeting, feeling of days past when thousands of people each day stepped ashore from small vessels.

Today the original Ellis Island reception center is a huge, brilliantly conceived museum that tells the story of the millions of immigrants who passed through the island on the way to becoming Americans. An estimated 100 million of today's Americans are descended from Ellis Island forebears.

The Ellis Island museum also traces the broader story of immigration—from the Native Americans to the present, and from the Asian Americans who landed on the West Coast to the Ellis Island "new" immigrants of the early twentieth century.

The museum's philosophy (as well as the essential goal of this book) is clearly delineated in the island's official guide, *Ellis Island and the Peopling of America*:

> It seems odd to call Native Americans immigrants since they have been established here so long. It also seems odd to speak of Puritans and other European newcomers to the Americas as immigrants; rather, we usually call them colonists or settlers. Likewise, we do not commonly speak of African Americans as immigrants, since most of them are descended from people brought forcibly from Africa as slaves many centuries ago.

Instead, we generally reserve immigrant for those who moved to the United States voluntarily during the nineteenth century and later, such as newcomers from places like Germany, Ireland, China, or the Dominican Republic.

Written United States history from about the end of the Civil War until the end of World War I tended to emphasize a highly prejudiced, provincial view that only

ELLIS ISLAND

Anglo-Saxons were worthy of the great American freedoms. Even a historian such as Woodrow Wilson, while still a professor at Princeton University, called immigrants of the late nineteenth century—from southern and eastern Europe—"men of the meaner sort." The Ellis Island museum reports that lopsided view of immigrants, but it also tells the story, often in their own words, of the courageous millions of brave people who left their ancient homelands and suffered miserable ocean voyages in quest of freedom and opportunity.

Powerful reasons made people leave their ancestral homes, whether in China or Italy. The great lure was the hope that their next location in the United States would be better. On the strength of that vision they turned their backs on ancient traditions and risked everything they had.

Although this volume concentrates on immigration to Ellis Island and the East Coast, the saga of nineteenth-century migrations is far broader than that. Great numbers of Asian Americans crossed the Pacific Ocean to enter the United States in the mid-nineteenth century, seeking fortunes in the California gold rush, building the first transcontinental railroad eastward from California, and establishing themselves as independent entrepreneurs.

Ellis Island has become the shining center of American immigration. Since 1982, the site has undergone a thorough restoration. Its exhibits accent Ellis Island of course, but the site also recounts all movements to the United States, from the Indians to the colonists, from the essentially Anglo-Saxon immigrants until about 1890 to the subsequent waves of so-called "new immigrants" from southern and eastern Europe, and the Asian Americans who entered the nation at ports bordering on the Pacific Ocean.

All of this is portrayed graphically in the museum, which in a very real sense is the national museum of immigration. The story is boldly displayed in the great hall and effectively extended in a myriad of small rooms that surround the hall. No person can leave the exhibits without a better sense of who we Americans really are, or without recognizing our debt to the millions of courageous people who endured fearsome ocean crossings for the chance to share in that concept of opportunity called America.

Between 1810 and 1925, nearly 40 million people left their homelands to come to the United States. They settled mainly in the cities, even though a great majority of them had been farmers in their native lands. Most of them lived quiet lives, but there also were such immigrants as Knute Rockne, the esteemed Notre Dame football coach; Bob Hope, the stellar comedian; Father Flanagan, founder of Boys Town; and Irving Berlin, whose hundreds of popular songs included, fittingly enough, "God Bless America."

Preface

As the nineteenth century neared an end, huge numbers of people were on the move everywhere in Europe, from villages to cities in their homelands, from nation to nation on the continent, and finally across the ocean to the United States. Millions of them also opted to go elsewhere—to Canada, Brazil, Argentina, Australia, and New Zealand.

However, this book concentrates on the immigrants who founded the colonies along the East Coast, then came to various East Coast ports until Castle Garden was opened in 1855, followed by the completion of Ellis Island in 1892. More than 70 percent of all newcomers entered this country via Castle Garden or Ellis Island. Mass immigration ended in 1924, when severe quotas were instituted.

Returning from the Statue of Liberty or Ellis Island to either New York or New Jersey intensifies the aura of the past. To pass under the upraised arm and the statue's calm visage without thinking of the days when millions of immigrants passed this symbol is to miss part of this mini-voyage.

One of the rarest experiences of my life came about ten years ago in late November, when I returned to the mainland after a day at Ellis Island. Darkness fell on the New York harbor shortly after 4 p.m. Millions of lights glowed in the windows of New York City's scintillating skyline. Miss Liberty's torch shone in the distant darkness and the lesser lights of Ellis Island seemed foreboding. On that little voyage I had the eerie feeling that, like my ancestors, my voyage into America was just beginning.

My destination was prosaic: to the New Jersey suburbs. But my imagination reverted to the 1890s, when poverty-stricken, often illiterate, and always fearful immigrants journeyed toward their dreams of freedom.

Chapter One

FROM THE BEGINNING: IMMIGRANTS ALL

Franklin Delano Roosevelt, 32nd president of the United States, erred in 1944 when he wrote, "All of our people, all over the country—except the pure-blooded Indians—are immigrants or descendants of immigrants, including even those who came over here on the Mayflower."

Actually, all Americans, even those now called "Native Americans," are immigrants or descended from immigrants. Thus, as Samuel Eliot Morison wrote, "what we mean by the history of the American people is the history of immigrants from other countries." We now know that the first Americans came from somewhere in present-day Siberia and traveled eastward toward the rising sun, or what in modern terms would be called "the promised land." Many years later, European treasure hunters sailed westward in the belief that there had to be a shorter, all-water route to the wealth of India. Along the way, those latter-day fortune seekers happened to find the Americas, North and South.

Those Indians of ancient times properly should be called the "Original Americans," for their ancestors, 20,000 years or so ago, crossed the Bering Strait on prehistoric islands (or perhaps a natural ice bridge). They left their lands in Asia and walked southward through what is now western Canada and the United States.

Why they left their ancestral homeland is not likely ever to be known. It might have been a single catastrophic event that made life intolerable or an extreme cold period in the wake of the glacial age. It might have been a powerful enemy that stormed out of Asia or it might have been starvation. Certainly these first Americans struggled onward, century after century, in the hope that eastward lay something warmer, something better, something safer. It would not have been a desire for riches; those primitive people sought the necessities of life rather than opulence.

The original Americans had all of the motivations that have ever since enticed settlers to migrate: The first tough decision was whether to leave their native villages or to stay. Those who left summoned the courage to face and endure incredible, unknown hardships, moving onward through uncertain, unmapped, and unknown terrain in quest of better lives. They were the vanguard of people linked in the emotional poem written in 1883 by Emma Lazarus—the words that immortalized forever "the tired, the poor, the hungry masses yearning to breathe free."

The journey of the Siberian tribes took thousands upon thousands of years. It is a story that never will be known fully because there is no written saga and even the dim oral legends have been changed by time. Certainly the migration paused for long times, perhaps decades, before moving on. Many, many generations of elders died along the way but new generations picked up the quest and journeyed on.

Entire tribes left the main stream of migration as the journey proceeded eastward. These defectors journeyed southward and crossed the North American Plains, settling as they went, and entered what is now called Mexico. They had reached as far as the southern tip of South America before the first European explorers began their search for a new and shorter route to the Indies. In western North America, those original people became the Pueblos, Cochimi, Apaches, Sioux, Navahos, Waiguri, Yaqui, Cheyennes, Crows, Osages, Pawnees, and many other tribes. The Pueblos set up North America's first permanent communities in cliffside "apartments."

About 10,000 to 12,000 years ago, that Indian migration finally reached the Atlantic Ocean, likely somewhere along what is now the Jersey Shore or perhaps on the banks of what is now New York Harbor. A broad region extending northward and eastward along the Atlantic Ocean became the home of the Algonquians, Iroquoians, Cherokees, Mohicans, Miamis, Choctaws, Seminoles, Tuscarorans, and the other tribes or nations that eventually spread from present-day Maine to Florida.

Those original Americans founded their own social orders, some warlike, others peaceful. They established their own forms of civilization in everything from cooking utensils to weapons and religions. Some became nomadic, hunting buffalo across the western plains; others, particularly the eastern Indians, farmed on the banks of streams and hunted in the dense woodlands. Although many established themselves permanently in definite areas, they believed the land was theirs to use but not to own forever.

They named their living sites after the terrain—Massachusetts, Cincinnati, Keokuk, Utah, Missouri, Arkansas, Poughkeepsie, Manhattan, Hoboken, Mississippi, Miami, Passaic, and on and on across the land they possessed.

Since those first settlers had no written language and thus no written history, their names for settlements and land forms eventually were written as interpreted by Europeans. It led often to ridiculous distortion or complete misinterpretations. As an example, the Passaic River in New Jersey has about 50 recorded spellings.

The first European explorers sailed westward seeking a short sea route to India, the storied land of gold, jewels, and spices. Inevitably, when they encountered lands unknown to Europeans, wishful thinking prompted them to believe that the territory was India. Ergo, the inhabitants of this new world had to be Indians. They quickly were labeled heathens, and as such they were believed to have little or no right to the land on which they had lived for thousands of years.

The explorers were harbingers of what immigration would bring to the New World in the way of diverse nationalities. It is believed that Norwegian Vikings, inspired by Lief Ericsson, had sought to colonize a bit of the North Atlantic region before the year 1000. The distance from their homeland and the miserable weather conditions forced them to abandon the effort.

Exploration had little to do with national pride. Christopher Columbus, an Italian, explored for Spain in 1492. The Italian Cabotos (Cabots), father Giovanni (John) and son Sebastian, sailed English vessels along the North Atlantic coast as early as 1498. Giovanni da Verrazano, an Italian, explored Newark Bay and the lower Hudson River for France in 1524, and Henry Hudson, an Englishman, sailed under a Dutch flag in 1609.

Columbus wrote that he had discovered "the New World" and other explorers used some variations on that theme. In an anomaly of fate, the two inter-connected huge land masses that explorers ultimately agreed blocked the way to the Indies were named for Amerigo Vespucci, who never captained a voyage of exploration.

Vespucci was an officer or passenger on several ships that looked in on the unnamed continent that is now South America. Totally ignoring the voyages of Columbus and others, he called the land he had seen "the New World" (as had Columbus).

When a new map appeared in 1507, its maker wrote: "Since Americus [Amerigo] Vespucci has discovered a fourth part of the world, it should be called after him . . . America." Every European nation except Spain and Portugal almost immediately adopted the name America for both the northern and southern continents. No magnet for European immigrants ever became more compelling than the single word, America.

Spain's claims to the New World were based on the voyages of Columbus. On his second voyage, Columbus left a small colony on New Hispaniola (the island of Haiti), but it was more a military outpost than a colony. Spanish conquests of Mexican Aztecs and Peruvian Incas and the subsequent shiploads of pirated gold headed for Spain later led to North American colonization through military outposts such as that at St. Augustine, begun in Florida in 1565. By 1776, Franciscan monks had extended Spanish settlements through Arizona, New Mexico, and on to the California coast.

The first genuine English colony intended to encourage migration was established by Sir Walter Raleigh, the well-known friend of England's Queen Elizabeth. Although the queen considered it madness to think that any English man or woman would travel 3,000 miles across a wild ocean to settle so far from England, she gave Raleigh broad powers in 1584 "to discover barbarous countries, not actually possessed of any Christian prince and inhabited by Christian people, to occupy and enjoy the same for ever."

A year later, Raleigh underwrote a colony on Roanoke Island in Virginia (now North Carolina) and sent 107 men to establish an English settlement. After a year of winter hardship, with few supplies and no women, the colonists returned to England.

A second expedition left for Roanoke Island in 1587, this time with 17 women and 11 children accompanying 89 men. Their leader, John White, returned to England to seek more supplies. Delayed two years by English fears of the Spanish Armada, White returned in 1591. The colony had vanished.

Finally, on May 13, 1607, three small ships entered Chesapeake Bay, then sailed up the James River to found Jamestown, Virginia. Despite several years of near-starvation, debilitating plagues, and troubles with the Indians, Jamestown endured. The colony proved that English immigrants, men and women alike, could live in the American wilderness despite severe obstacles that should have crippled or killed off the colony.

Within three years, Holland sent its first people to the New World in about 1610, essentially to establish a fur trade with the native people. The Dutch based their claim to American territory on the voyage in 1609 of Henry Hudson on the *Half Moon.* Much of Hudson's fame rests on a detailed journal of the voyage kept by fellow Englishman and First Mate Robert Juet. It memorialized Hudson's exploration and fanned the flames of a Dutch colonization effort that lasted only slightly more than 45 years.

Hudson first encountered the mainland at what is now Delaware Bay. After his ship "strooke" a bar in the bay in August, he forsook the Delaware as a possible route to India. He returned to the Atlantic Ocean and coasted slowly northward along what is now New Jersey. Juet noted the islands and inlets along the coast and, as the *Half Moon* neared what is now Sandy Hook Bay, he became a mildly poetic spokesman for the region: "This is a very good land to fall with, and a pleasant land to see."

After sailing up the river that now bears his name, Hudson was thwarted by rockstrewn, shallow falls near what is now Albany. Aware that this was not the water route to India either, he returned to Manhattan, ordered full sails to be broken out, and continued to Holland, where Juet's journal excited the greed of the Dutch East India Company, Hudson's sponsor.

Especially intriguing to Dutch East Indies stockholders was Juet's description of the Palisades, the towering basaltic cliff on the west side of the Hudson River. The cliff had been cast high by a volcano of a hundred million years before. Dutch sponsors generally ignored Juet's descriptions of the fine land he saw, preferring to concentrate on his description of the "white green" cliff on the west side of the river that perhaps held a "copper or silver mine."

Hollanders intent on settling began arriving at the island the Indians called Man-a-hat-ta (Heavenly Land) in 1614 and by 1616 had sent exploration parties southward along the Jersey Shore, then northward up the Delaware River as far north as what is now Philadelphia. Dutch colonization did not have a solid base until 1626, when Peter Minuit made his famed purchase of the island of Man-a-hat-ta from the Indians in exchange for trinkets and baubles later estimated to be worth $24 in the currency of that time.

Gold and other riches, rather than permanent agrarian settlement, continued to dominate European exploration for decades. The basic clue to desultory Dutch colonization is found in the charter for the Dutch West India Company, incorporated in 1625. It had two specific objects: to capture gold-laden Spanish galleons and to establish a fur trade with the Indians—in that order. That charter did not mention colonization; there was little thought of permanent settlement.

West India Company stockholders stirred restlessly over the relatively poor returns from furs. One report showed that furs brought in only 6,000 guilders, compared with 6 million guilders from pirating Spanish vessels. Directors thereupon protested a possible peace treaty with Spain, scornfully referring to promises of peacetime colonization as merely "a trifling trade with the Indians."

The first threat to Dutch domination of the Middle Atlantic region came in 1638 when two small vessels from Sweden, the *Kalmar Nyckel* and the *Vogal Grip*, sailed into Delaware Bay. Intriguingly, they were commanded by Peter Minuit, the Dutchman who 13 years before had bought Manhattan Island for his home country, Holland.

New Amsterdam and New Sweden carried on a desultory, at times almost comic, warfare for control of the Delaware River. Neither had sufficient numbers of colonists or a system of colonization to strengthen their tenuous holds on the land. Both awaited the inevitable day when England would make its first major effort to claim America—all of it—as its own.

The colony at Jamestown was a mere small first step toward England's major moves to make America its own. In 1632, after spending five years trying to colonize on a Newfoundland peninsula, Sir George Calvert made a bold request for a new American location. King Charles I gave his good friend, best known in history as Lord Baltimore, a grant that extended from the latitude of Philadelphia to the north bank of the Potomac River. The site was carved from Virginia, a haphazard clerical mistake that precipitated a fishing rights disagreement between Virginia and Maryland that endured for more than three centuries.

Calvert had been converted to Roman Catholicism and had been proclaimed Baron Baltimore in the Irish peerage. His grant gave him full right to prosper from sales of his land—plus the right to rule. Calvert named his colony Maryland to honor the

Virgin Mary. The Baltimore lands sold well, giving the Calvert family one of the first fortunes made in America. In Maryland, as in Rhode Island and later Pennsylvania, religious tolerance became an actuality.

England would always maintain that the voyages of the Cabots gave them an unassailable claim on all the New World, despite the fact that the Italian father and son never sailed south of what is now New Jersey. The early attempts at settlement in Virginia were lackluster. Then, in 1620, English Puritans founded the enduring Massachusetts Colony, which looked to Heaven rather than England for sanction of its enterprise.

The Puritans were Separatists—worshipers who had separated from the Church of England. They received colonizing sanction of a sort in 1620 through a charter from Virginia (which then included all American land north to present-day Massachusetts). The original intention was to establish a trading post at the mouth of the Hudson River, then well within Virginia's territorial claims.

In the early autumn of 1620, the little band of Puritans trooped aboard the *Mayflower*, probably the best known of all colonial vessels. After a horrible crossing of 64 days in the stormy North Atlantic, the *Mayflower* dropped anchor on November 9 in the harbor at what is now Provincetown at the tip of Cape Cod. Since the location was outside of the Virginia claim, it was declared that "when they came ashore they would use their own liberty, for none had the right to command them." The bold attitude might be interpreted as the first defiance not only of Virginia and sectarian authority in general but of England as well.

Finding the tip of Cape Cod incapable of supporting life, the Puritans decided to settle at Plymouth, so-named by Virginia's much-traveled coastal explorer, Captain John Smith. One hundred and two men, women, and children disembarked on the frozen coast on December 16, fully aware that they faced a dreadful winter. Their worst imaginings were more than matched.

They built crude huts to fend off some of the bitter cold, but almost immediately after they landed, a "great sickness" decimated the tiny outpost. Only 50 settlers survived. Despite the rigors of weather, awesome death totals, and near-terror in the first winter, not one survivor asked to board the *Mayflower* when it returned to England in April.

Later, however, some of the original Massachusetts leaders and their families left the rigid, uncompromising Puritan village, moving outward into Rhode Island, Connecticut, and Long Island, seeking freedoms that the Puritan fathers were not willing to grant.

The Massachusetts Bay Colony, established in 1630, encouraged migration to America. Simultaneously, the failure of many crops and England's preoccupation with the Thirty Years War cut off trade with the European continent. About 20,000 English colonists arrived in New England between 1620 and 1650.

On June 24, 1664, King Charles II gave a huge portion of land in the middle of the East Coast to his brother James, the Duke of York, who in turn bestowed the tract on a pair of court favorites, Lord John Berkeley and Sir George Carteret. The land centered on New Amsterdam and included all of both the modern states called New York and New Jersey. New Amsterdam was renamed New York to honor the duke.

In March 1664, England dispatched a small fleet of four ships and an invasion force of 400 men to subdue both New Amsterdam and New Sweden. The Dutch and the Swedes quickly surrendered and in the minds of Englishmen, all of America belonged to John Bull. Astonishingly, and in a foretelling of what Manhattan (and all of America) would become, the British invaders found that New Amsterdam's citizens spoke a total of 18 different languages—including Dutch, English, Swedish, Finnish, French, Norwegian, Spanish, Portuguese, Czech, Danish, Italian, German, and Polish.

In 1675, the first Quakers in America established a town they called Salem in southern New Jersey—six years before William Penn founded Philadelphia, his City of Brotherly Love. The Quakers spread through southern New Jersey and Pennsylvania, augmented in Pennsylvania by German Protestants invited by Penn to share the province. The first Germans arrived in 1683, the forerunners of thousands of Pietists, Mennonites, Amish, Dunkers, Lutherans, Calvinists, and Moravians. Generally all of these German groups were lumped into the single, erroneous name "Pennsylvania Dutch," a corruption of "Deutsch," or German.

Fundamental in the story of migration to American are the ships in which the newcomers rode westward from Europe, beginning with the high-decked colonial ships such as the *Mayflower* or the *Kalmar Nyckel*, each cited because replicas of them are berthed in northeastern ports—the *Mayflower* in Plymouth, Massachusetts, and the *Kalmar Nyckel* in Wilmington, Delaware. To go below on either of those one-time state-of-the-art sailing ships is to stir the imagination. Anyone over 5 feet tall is in danger of striking his forehead on overhead beams.

The limited deck space on a colonial vessel would have been crowded with farm animals, animal food, bits of furniture, balled fruit trees, and farm equipment. Each passenger could bring some favored thing from home, a constant feature of immigration through all time. Below decks there was no privacy, no toilet facilities, no storage space, and only the crudest of cooking possibilities. In that unsanitary hold they slept, bore children, and kept themselves as clean as possible. The thought of spending months aboard such a vessel is enough to invoke claustrophobia and disbelief.

Compounding the woes were the crude navigation aids and the never completely-dismissed notion that the ocean held ferocious, giant beasts, capable of capsizing a vessel. Worse, who knew for sure that the earth was round? Hardships were accepted stoically, as part of the price that those leaving home were expected to accept in the name of their religious beliefs.

Historian Samuel Eliot Morison in his *Oxford History of the American People* repeated an account of a colonial voyage written by an immigrant named Gottlieb Mittelberger, on his way to Philadelphia in 1750:

> Bad drinking water and putrid salt meat, excessive heat and crowding, lice so thick they could be scraped off the body, seas so rough that hatches were battened down and everyone vomited in the foul hold; passengers succumbing to dysentery, scurvy, canker, and mouth-rot.

It is vital to remember that these colonial immigrants—driven from their homes by religious persecution, imprisonment for debt, or the fear of starvation on European lands they never could hope to own—were the courageous and the bold, the dissenters, the political prisoners, the rebels, the cantankerous, the survivors, and those willing to gamble that whatever they found in America would be far better than anything they had ever known. Those traits describe most immigrants in all times.

More than anything, the great wonder of the New World was the vastness of the land, occupied initially only by scattered Native American tribes. The natives "sold" the land at bargain prices—making their marks on agreements since they could not write, and asking such trivial pay as beads, trinkets, blankets, guns, and alcohol. The Indians may even have had the gleeful thought that they were merely renting the land, not deeding the acres in perpetuity to the invading newcomers.

By 1680, six of the original 13 colonies were owned by individual proprietors, all favorites of England's ruling family. The proprietors were essentially real estate salesmen with the power to exploit some of the greatest land opportunities ever offered at minimum prices. They received land from the crown, outright or for trifling annual rents such as one peppercorn or a few shillings. They could sell the land or rent it for annual fees. Most such proprietors never left England and had only the vaguest of notions about their holdings. As often as not, new settlers merely moved away from settled proprietary regions and squatted on the land, ignoring fees and boldly resisting efforts to collect them. These immigrants slowly were becoming a totally new breed, heady with the notion that whoever tilled the soil owned the land.

With the exception of the African Americans, kidnapped in Africa and herded aboard ships like so many beasts of burden, or white prisoners taken from their English cells and pushed into America-bound ships, the immigrants embarked of their own free will to seek religious or economic freedom.

The Africans who were driven from home at gunpoint certainly were not willing emigrants, who by definition initiated the steps to move to a new land. The bewildered Africans were the imports of greedy land owners eager to escape the labor in their own fields. The first slaves were introduced into Virginia in 1619, and rapid growth of southern cotton plantations was the excuse for the wicked trade in human lives.

Slaves transported to the New World were chained and put aboard foul ships bound for both North and South America. They slept like so many logs, piled side by side to get the highest possible number of bodies aboard. They were fed as little food as possible on voyages that lasted as long as three months from port to port. About one in five of the imprisoned victims died and high percentages of the rest arrived in American ports weakened and emaciated. By the time of the Civil War, nearly four million slaves had labored all their lives on southern plantations. America for them was neither the land of the free nor the shining symbol of opportunity.

Proprietors brought to the immigrant scene an element that became vital in all the great waves of immigration: written propaganda to induce settlers to brave the wild Atlantic Ocean. Seeking to sell some of the huge acreage that King Charles II had given them, the East New Jersey Proprietors hired George Scot in 1685 as possibly the first publicist to sell America to prospective immigrants. He wrote a pamphlet with double objectives: to get buyers for East New Jersey land (which he had never seen) and to entice experienced tradesmen to the New World, where their skills were desperately needed. Scot succumbed to his own blandishments and died in 1685 aboard a ship bound for New Jersey.

Scot's pamphlet established two elements that would always color the immigrant experience—powerful and sometimes wildly exaggerated propaganda to entice new immigrants to leave their homelands, and a stress on the good livelihoods skilled hands could expect if they dared the arduous crossing of the Atlantic Ocean.

After extolling the East Jersey climate ("like Naples," he wrote in an absurd stretching of the truth), Scot told of towering forests, fertile fields, ample fish and game, and rich black soil that yielded "great burthens of corn." He unblushingly wrote that "from an apple-tree-seed in four years, without grafting, there sprang a tree that in the fourth year bore such a quantity of apples as yielded a barrel of cider."

Parts of the New Jersey paradise were available for small annual rents, Scot said; it behooved Englishmen to snap up the land bargains. Scot pointed out that the proprietors offered the chance for artisans and craftsmen to earn the land by working off a four-year bond, using their God-given skills. If the proprietors paid a man's transportation, the four years of work would be rewarded with "30 acres, 2 pence the acre [rent] and so much corn as will sow 2 acres, a cow and a sow."

Anyone willing to pay his own way could get the same land benefits and the proprietors would "oblige themselves to find them work for a year, after their arrival, at as good Rates as they have here [in England], until they can furnish themselves with some stock to make better advantage upon the Place." Scot's final pitch was to tradesmen and craftsmen: "All Sorts of Tradesmen may make a brave Lively-hood there, such as carpenters, Ship-wrights, Rope-makers, Smiths, Brick-makers, Taylors, Tanners, Cowpers [coopers], Mill-wrights, Joyners, Shoo makers, and any such like."

Scot's propaganda had three important elements. For the first time, it emphasized that work was vital to success in America, in marked contrast to the original emphasis on seeking easy wealth in the New World. Secondly, it underscored the vital need for skilled workers in an emerging nation. Third, it was one of the first efforts to encourage immigration for reasons other than religion or other basic freedoms.

A century later, as the fateful 1770s approached, inhabitants in America's 13 colonies were mainly English, Irish, and Scotch, with large numbers of Germans, French, and Scandinavians. Immigrants from southern and eastern Europe were extremely rare.

Even more marked among Americans was the schism in religions: Puritans, Congregationalists, Presbyterians, Episcopalians, Quakers, Baptists, Anabaptists, Dutch Reformed, Swedish Lutherans, German Lutherans, French Huguenots, Moravians, Amish, a few Methodists, and many other splintered Protestant sects (especially in Pennsylvania), and, except for Maryland, small numbers of Roman Catholics (generally, and scornfully, known to Protestants as Papists).

By the time of the American Revolution, descendants of the first settlers had lived in America for nearly 150 years. Every one of them was an immigrant or descended directly from one or more immigrants. Many of them had nostalgic feelings for the Old Country but few of them ever considered an eastward journey to revive the life they or their ancestors had led. Those who were of English descent had little allegiance to King George III, particularly the Scotch and Irish Presbyterians. They had become Americans, a new breed of independent, confident people, eager for a government in which they shared. Never before had there been such a nation.

Immigration was an established facet of American life by the time the Declaration of Independence was signed. By then, about 2.5 million European immigrants or their direct descendants lived in the emerging country. Among the charges in the Declaration of Independence was a clear recognition that a unique new nation had come into being:

> He has endeavoured to prevent the population of these states; for that purpose obstructing the Laws for the Naturalization of Foreigners; refusing to pass others to encourage their migrations hither; and raising the conditions of new Appropriations of Lands.

Chapter Two

A NATION BUILT ON IMMIGRANT BACKS

Hemmed in on the west by the foreboding Appalachian Mountains ranging from Maine to Georgia, the infant United States desperately needed a solid and widespread economy to make it truly independent from England. States north of Delaware sought it in factories built to use the power of swiftly-moving streams. States to the south sought it in huge cotton plantations.

Both regions would need ever-swelling streams of immigrant workers from abroad—willing immigrants from the British Isles and northern Europe to man the water-powered factories; kidnapped African slaves to work the southern cotton fields. Eventually the disparate economies would clash in the great Civil War.

Few immigrants came to America—about 5,000 each year—in the decade following the adoption of the United States Constitution and the election of George Washington as President. It was not a matter of officially opposing newcomers; on Thanksgiving Day in 1795 President George Washington asked Americans to pray that their new nation might become "more and more a safe and propitious asylum for the unfortunate of other countries."

Two years later, a worried Congressman argued that the United States would have to cease its policy of unregulated immigration, lest the nation be overrun by foreigners. He felt that the United States had reached maturity and that it could not afford any increases in population. Those opposite viewpoints would create battle lines that would rage through all American history. They still resound in today's emotions concerning immigrants, whether legal or illegal.

The War of 1812 cruelly showed the deficiencies of a nation bogged down beside crude dirt roads and small, erratically-run water-powered factories. The nation needed to create a sound infrastructure and needed more workers to build it. Increased immigration was the answer. Coincidentally, the Napoleonic era in Europe, followed by the awesome tragedy in Ireland's potato fields, quickened the pace.

Only 120,000 newcomers came from Europe in the 1820s; in the 1830s the number swelled to 540,000, of whom 44 percent were Irish, 30 percent German, and 15 percent English. The totals rose rapidly in the 1840s when 1,700,000 immigrants arrived and reached an early tidal flood in the 1850s when 2,814,554 foreigners came to America.

Many of these pre–Civil War immigrants were Irish country laborers escaping from the horrors of the well-known potato famines. In the five-year period after 1845, more than a million Irish men, women, and children died from starvation in Ireland. Hundreds of thousands of the survivors found their way to seaports, scraping together coins to take ships for London, or, increasingly, boarding sailing ships bound for America. The cost of steerage to New York was $40 for adults and $20 for children, not inconsiderable funds for nearly-hopeless, nearly-penniless survivors.

Unscrupulous and wealthy English leaders in Ireland recognized that they could rid themselves of starving, homeless people—English and Irish alike—by paying for their passage to America. They rationalized that America had the will and the money to support these poor, uneducated new immigrants. Some towns emptied their prisons and almshouses by giving occupants tickets to the New World.

Despite the brutal oppression at home, leaving one's village was a wrenching experience. Even the walk to the seaports over dusty or muddy roads, depending on the season, brought death to many. Thieves lurked along the way, hoping to steal what little these wretched people had. At the ports, immigrants had to bargain for passage to America, promising nearly anything to get aboard a decrepit, disease-infected sailing ship waiting to ferry them across the Atlantic.

Helpless, homeless, and mostly illiterate because Roman Catholic children were not permitted to attend public schools controlled by Protestant leaders, they knew nothing of maps or geography. Their knowledge of America usually rested on a letter someone in their village had received from an Irishman who had gone to America earlier. If the would-be immigrants wondered about the potential hazards of the upcoming voyage, their information was likely to come from cruel and ignorant sailors met at dockside.

Truly these were the "huddled masses" that Emma Lazarus would write about decades later. They faced horrible overcrowding in the bowels of each ship, quartered so deep down they were near the steering mechanism of a ship (and thus they, and all who would follow them became known as "steerage" passengers). Generally their bunks were merely rough wooden platforms covered with straw. Food was scarce. No medicines or doctors were available: a sick passenger had two alternatives—an agonizing death or a body-wracking survival.

Sailing ships averaged about ten weeks to cross the North Atlantic Ocean, but winter gales and icebergs could throw any of the smaller ships wildly off course.

Passengers were warned to take 60 days' worth of food centered on such things as legumes, oatmeal, tea, flour, and other non-perishables. Ship-furnished food in those days of non-refrigeration was rotten, horrible tasting, or both.

Despite laws intended to lessen overcrowding, enterprising, if evil, shipping companies would load an established number at one port, then sail to another port and cram another hundred or so people in on top of the legal number. Each passenger was seen as so much miscellaneous cargo; the more in steerage, the richer the shipping company became.

Faced with the overcrowding, the detestable food, the certainty of unrelenting seasickness, and the overwhelming threat of such diseases as diarrhea, trench mouth, and scurvy, as well as measles and cholera, it is a source of wonder that only about one in every ten passengers died. On some of the English ships transporting Irish immigrants, almost a quarter of the passengers died. Such boats were often called "coffin ships" as a grim reminder of the conditions the captains perpetuated.

Only a few letters tell of the crossings of this period, but a portion of one from a Sussex, England woman, written in May 1828, told of one:

> I will not grieve your hearts with all our sufferings, for my paper will not hold it. Little Mary was very ill with the fever that so many died with—seven children and one woman. . . . If you know of any coming here tell them never to come where the vessel is so full; for we was shut down in darkness for a fortnight till so many died; then the hatch was opened. . . .

Nearly all the immigrants of the 1840s and 1850s went ashore in Boston, New York, or Baltimore, with New York far and away the most favored site. The arriving foreigners faced little examination in America except for a cursory health check aboard each vessel at the debarkation point. Examiners overlooked the emaciation of passengers and the filthy accommodations, concerning themselves mainly with such contagious diseases as smallpox, typhoid fever, and cholera.

After each passenger was hastily checked, the ship's log was studied for deaths at sea or evidence of epidemic diseases. Once that was completed, the vessel could dock and passengers were hustled ashore as quickly as possible. Swarms of con men converged on the bewildered immigrants, seeking to fleece them. With several miles of docks lining both sides of the Hudson River in New York Harbor, it was impossible for police to protect the immigrants.

Wherever immigrants came ashore in every East Coast state, authorities especially feared that the newcomers might become public burdens—a fear that ran through all immigration procedures until Ellis Island closed halfway through the twentieth century. At first, some states sought bonds to insure that an individual might never become a public charge. Few immigrants could post such a bond and ultimately a simple admission tax was usually levied on each immigrant.

There was plenty of work in the United States for the immigrants, although most of it was menial. Earlier arrivals, from the 1820s and 1830s, often helped countrymen who came later, usually unselfishly but sometimes asking outrageously high fees for their services. The Irish also eventually edged into city politics, especially in Boston and New York, where politicians had a corner on jobs, most of which were low-paid duties for women in households or hard labor for males.

By 1790, the first United States Census revealed about four million people living in America, or more exactly, the eastern part of North America. Most of the 1.5 million additional Americans since 1770 had been born in this country. A few had pushed westward beyond the Allegheny Mountains, presaging the westward movement that in time would send swarms of people outward to the Mississippi River and far beyond.

In 1830, the population of the United States was 13 million. Thirty years later, in 1860, as the North and the South began squaring off for the Civil War, about 39 million people lived in the nation. Those 30 years saw America grow from a nation of blacksmith shops and little one-man or two-man manufactories to the emergence of a powerful industrial nation linked by railroads and canals.

Immigrant hands and muscles were no longer needed to fell the forests and till the soil but to dig the canal ditches and to spread the ballast and lay the wooden ties and steel railroad tracks that by 1840 had begun to knit the nation together.

Coincidentally, economic conditions for European peasants plunged from bad to wretched. Travelers' accounts between 1830 and 1850 persistently recounted the dreadful, unsanitary hovels in which most Irish farm families lived in the Old Country. Irish laborers and farm workers seldom acquired any money; most were paid "in conacre," which meant the right to work a potato patch the following year. Life in Ireland's city slums was, if anything, worse. Education offered no hope; young Irish Catholic boys and girls were not accepted in public schools controlled by Protestants.

Young Irishmen streamed toward the docks, seeking passage to America. Between 1815 and 1845, more than 850,000 Irish emigrants headed westward to America. Then came the dreadful potato famine, an appalling phenomenon almost beyond comparison with any other natural disaster. Between 1846 and 1854, a million and a quarter Irish men and women left their storied land for America. More than a million stayed behind to die.

A Nation Built on Immigrant Backs

Completion of New York State's Erie Canal in 1812 signalled a new era of shipment on man-made waterways. New Jersey built two canals to link the Pennsylvania coal mines with New York City. Pennsylvania built a canal system that extended from its eastern regions to Pittsburgh. The ingenious canal builders and proprietors took canal boats up and over the Allegheny Mountains at an elevation of 2,300 feet—almost a half mile—on inclined planes, on which water-powered winches hauled barges from waterway to waterway along the mountain face.

The factory system for cotton spinning and weaving became firmly established in New England as a result of the War of 1812. There had been so little domestic weaving in the United States that the factory system was introduced without conflict. By 1840 there were 1,200 cotton mills in the United States operating 2,250,000 spindles, two-thirds of them in New England. Power looms were being manufactured in large numbers, and even exported.

Immigrants, particularly young Irish women, found menial, routine work in the woolen and cotton factories in all mill areas north of Philadelphia. The poet Ralph Greenleaf Whittier once had praised New England's mill girls as the "fair unveiled Nuns of Industry." By the 1840s, those "fair Nuns" had been replaced by Irish girls, wan and pallid from their years as victims of the potato debacle in their native land. Woefully underpaid, these mill workers lived in abject poverty in shacks near the mills.

Massive numbers of Irish pick-and-shovel workers were needed to shovel the earth. Employers plied them with liquor, in the common belief that Irishmen craved alcohol more than food. Untold numbers of these hapless immigrants died, from epidemics of such diseases as cholera, from the effects of alcohol, and from exposure to the chills of winter and the relentless sun of summer. Most of them were buried in unmarked graves beside the tracks, without sentiment or ceremony, left for passing years to erase even memories of them.

Despite their lives as farmers in Ireland, most of the Irish immigrants headed for the cities, hoping that after the toil in the canals and on the railroads, they could find their fortunes in city industry or along the docks of major ports such as New York City or Boston. They huddled together in city slums every bit as dreadful as the farm huts they had abandoned in their flight to America. They were nearly all poor, untutored, but proud, often sustained only by their Roman Catholic churches. They were scorned by earlier immigrants from other countries and maligned by city newspapers. Altogether, they were considered at best a joke or a comical nuisance, at worst a scourge—necessary, but disreputable.

When a cholera epidemic hit Newark, New Jersey in 1832, the editor of the *Newark Sentinel of Freedom* pointed out that most of the initial deaths were in John Sharkey's house near the city wharf, a lodging place for Irish laborers, "the most filthy the town affords." The *Sentinel* offered this vivid portrayal:

> In a house containing four rooms not much over ten feet square each, and in a hovel adjoining, were stored nearly thirty individuals, as stated residents. Others, to what numbers unknown, made it a rendezvous for carousals. Among such a community, guilty of all kinds of excesses, and surrounded by filth, it would not be at all surprising that disease should be engendered, even without the existence of a foreign cause.

The editor of the *Newark Daily Advertiser* reported on July 13, 1832 that Newark officials raided Sharkey's, carting 24 people to a barracks a half mile away and leaving them "to live or to die." The editor scolded city officials for such behavior, even in an emergency, calling the action "inhuman and cruel in the extreme." However, like all officialdom, he listed the cholera victims as "Irish" or "Colored," with the clear implication that such people were cholera's scourge. By early August, when "some of the most respected friends" of the editor began to die, he agreed that the cause was not solely the fault of immigrants.

The first major break with President George Washington's hope for tolerance of immigrants came in the 1840s and 1850s. At first, in the 1840s, rampaging mobs of "nativists" beat Irish immigrants and burned Catholic churches. The anti-immigrant movement gained both strength and organization when the secret Order of the Star Spangled Banner was formed. Membership was limited to native-born Protestants. Members, when questioned about the group by outsiders, were taught to respond, "I know nothing."

Inevitably this anti-Catholic and anti-immigrant power sought political representation as the Native American party, although it found the euphemism "Know Nothing" was generally its lot. In the 1854 elections, the Know Nothings almost won New York state and did control Massachusetts, electing a wholly new legislature.

The group reverted to a bullying, physical presence, such as threatening voters with small weapons and, in Baltimore, with a loaded cannon backed by rowdies. "Know Nothings" nominated aged Millard Fillmore for President in 1856. That bid failed, the movement collapsed, and was finished by the time the Civil War began.

Yet when the immigrant survivors wrote home, they usually neglected to describe, or overlooked, the hardships of the crossings, the unhappy receptions in the cities, and the desperation in most of their lives. They considered themselves Americans and by choice, urban workers and residents, freed from the fields and for the first time in many of their lives, proud of the few coins in their pockets.

The canals and railroads, added to the rough roads leading through passes in the Allegheny Mountains, hastened the movement of settlers into the western lands of Ohio, Tennessee, Kentucky, and other open areas as far as the Mississippi River and beyond.

The early village called Cleveland grew to a mighty Lake Erie port by 1850. Cincinnati by that time boasted a population of 115,000. New Orleans was a thriving port town by 1840 and in the mid 1830s the frontier town of Chicago was averaging better than a lake vessel nearly every working day around the calendar. Many west-bound immigrants streamed into all the cities, seeking work, although most Irish immigrants continued to settle in northeastern cities.

Two hectic years in mid-century quickly threw the situation into stark perspective. In 1848, 189,176 immigrants landed in New York City. Two years later, in 1850, 212,796 newcomers arrived—117,088 Irishmen, 45,035 Germans, and 50,223 from other lands. Most astonishingly, in that year 1,912 ships sailed into the harbor laden with immigrants in steerage—an average of about five new immigrant ships every day throughout the year.

German immigrants came in droves during the 1848 revolution in their native land. They were mainly peasants, although the political refugees in 1848 included many German philosophers and other intellectuals who loved the exciting stimulus of New York City. Westward across the Hudson River, Hoboken, New Jersey became a strong German waterfront community; nearby Newark gave German beermakers a major center; and German migrants moved westward to found substantial enclaves in Cincinnati, St. Louis, and Milwaukee.

The pre–Civil War waves of immigrants enhanced the wealth and well-being of America but the immigrants often were detested, partially for religious reasons but also because many of the Irish were willing to work for lower wages and tolerated lower work standards. The continuing influx of Irish immigrants won them voting power, particularly in New York City, where first-generation Irish immigrants accounted for 34 percent of all voters. With voting power came representation; the Irish were near the top when politicians handed out city jobs.

Despite the help accorded many immigrants by countrymen who had preceded them to America, it grew increasingly evident that large numbers of immigrants were being subjected to cheating and dishonesty, ranging from theft of the pitifully tiny sums of money they were able to squirrel into America to cases of beatings and rape. The first step toward bringing a semblance of order to the admission of foreign-born people came from necessity and group compassion. Germans had organized an American immigrant society as early as 1784 and in 1841 the more powerful Irish Emigrant Society was organized.

In 1847 the two emigrant groups joined forces to convince New York state to create a Board of Commissioners of Emigration on May 5. This new ten-member body included six members appointed by the New York governor, the mayors of New York City and Brooklyn, and the presidents of the Irish and German Emigrant Societies. In its first year the commissioners established the Emigrant Hospital and Refuge on Ward's Island in New York City, where immigrants suffering from non-contagious diseases could be treated.

The situation grew increasingly intolerable as ever-growing numbers of immigrant ships sailed into the harbor. Inspectors could no longer keep up with the task of boarding every ship and examining every immigrant. The checks of the immigrants were so fleeting as to be almost laughable. In 1890, when the ships docked, there was no protection for the newly arrived people. Police departments had neither the will nor the manpower to keep up with the mounting problems.

Surprisingly, perhaps even amazingly, the national government took only the mildest actions for more than a century after the Declaration of Independence was adopted. The sole actions, both in 1798, were provoked by fears that trouble might be stirred by free-thinking French emigrants streaming in from the West Indies, along with a few Irishmen fleeing the Irish Revolution of 1798. A Naturalization Act extended the required period for citizenship from five to fourteen years. The Sedition Act, in force for only two years, gave the President the power to eject suspected foreigners by executive decree.

Thus as the nation's borders extended to the Pacific Ocean with the Louisiana Purchase in 1804 and to Mexico after the Mexican War, hundreds of thousands of immigrants left the docks in New York, boarded trains, and followed previous colonial descendants to western lands purchased from speculators. Immigrants were an accepted facet of America as far as the Mississippi River and just beyond by the start of the Civil War. By 1870 they were a factor in Pacific coast affairs. They had become a national matter of concern and a matter of how to assimilate this "different" type of immigrant.

New York City had by far the most to gain, and, as a corollary, the most to lose from immigration controls. Two-thirds of all immigrants from 1786 to the opening of Ellis Island in 1792 entered via New York City. After that, the concentration was for decades even more intense.

In streamed the flood of immigrants. Little more was done for them or to them than a head count and a very quick eyeball check for diseases. Once a ship debarked them and they headed down the gangplank into the vast area of America, they were not even required to have a simple visa or rudimentary passport. Superficially, then, almost as soon as the immigrants passed the simple inspection on ship or at dockside, they could be considered as "American" as anyone they passed on the street. The swindlers and the thieves knew the difference; the immigration process threw immigrants to such wolves.

Liverpool, LeHavre, and Hamburg were the early major ports of embarkation. European governments tried with little success to ease the problems of leaving. Some also sought, with no great improvement, to require ship owners to enforce a minimum of space, rations, and decent treatment in steerage.

New York—and the nation—desperately needed a large, well-appointed center where immigrants could be landed, inspected, classified, housed, and protected. Such a place would protect the entering foreigners and prepare them for the towns and states toward which they would head. Such a place had to be on water linked to European traffic lanes, of course. To allow docking and disembarking, it had to be commodious enough to hold thousands of people at one time, and it had to be in a section of the city where the people could be directed into the streets with at least a modicum of protection.

Simply put, there seemed to be no such existing place in New York City—and upstate rural New York legislators could never be induced to pour money into New York City to build such a haven for foreigners.

Then, suddenly, with almost breathtaking serendipity, the opportunity for a splendid immigration depot presented itself in 1854, in a location the city fully owned. The private managers of the esteemed city-owned Castle Garden, who had been renting the site for 15 years to provide world-class entertainment for New York's elite, decided not to renew their lease on the property.

The decision came as a surprise. The city had been at work for two years improving and enlarging adjacent Battery Park. Thousands of wagonloads of coal ashes, construction scrap, and miscellaneous rubbish more than doubled the size of the park. In the process, the space between Castle Garden's island and the mainland was filled in.

Immigrant officials quickly saw the opportunity: Castle Garden could become the commodious, perfectly-located place for a splendid new immigration depot. If revered Castle Garden could be acquired for that purpose, New York City would have the finest immigration center in the world.

Chapter Three

THE CASTLE OF DREAMS

Castle Garden began as a huge circular stone structure hastily built in 1807 as a fort (the West Battery), when fears were rife that sometime soon British frigates and battleships would sail up the broad bay and set troops ashore on New York City's exposed and unprotected lower end—The Battery. The fort's 28 guns could sweep the harbor and, with cannon in another fort on nearby Governor's Island, ward off potential enemy attacks. The British never came. As a fort, the sturdy stone building was useless.

New York City acquired the fort in 1824 and New Yorkers renamed the former fortress Castle Clinton to honor acclaimed New York Governor DeWitt Clinton.

A handsome green woodland, interspersed with broad walking paths, covered the mainland north of the fort, giving credence to the word Park that had been added to The Battery's name. Handsome houses lined streets leading northward toward Wall Street. Residents warmly approved the army evacuation and the roofing over of the fort in 1845 to provide an elegant, privately-run music hall, capable of seating 6,000 ticket holders. Appropriately, the building was renamed Castle Garden.

Wealthy patrons left their carriages on the mainland and crossed a stretch of water on a long stone bridge that linked Castle Garden to the mainland. The world's greatest actors, actresses, opera notables, acrobats, and musical groups entertained capacity crowds. Of all the notable entertainers, the name most often associated with the Castle Garden was that of "The Swedish Nightingale" Jenny Lind, who gave her first concert in America in the hall on September 11, 1850. The Lind concert, sponsored by the great impresario Phineas T. Barnum, spread the name Castle Garden across the nation.

Within less than four years after the Lind concert, however, Castle Garden had lost its charm as an entertainment palace. It required only modest imagination to see that the imposing vacant old fort/music hall, if properly presented and properly refurbished, could become the prime site for an immigration depot.

The proposed depot would face the magnificent harbor, would allow docking to receive immigrants, had a building large enough to accommodate thousands of people, and was in a section of the city that was relatively protected from spurious immigrant chasers. New York City needed only permission from the New York legislature to make a deal with the federal government.

Precious months slid away before legislators gathered in Albany on April 13, 1855, to approve use of the site as an immigration facility to process the foreigners before they left New York for widely spread areas of the United States. Three weeks later, the commissioners and the city signed a four-year lease on the site.

The wealthiest, trend-setting neighbors were moving northward as the city grew away from Battery Park, but storms of protest erupted among the remaining 30,000 residents of the fashionable First Ward, in which Castle Garden stood. They sought—and got—a temporary injunction in the Superior Court.

Noted railroad financier Cornelius Vanderbilt, who had not yet moved away, wrote from his mansion at 5 Bowling Green that summer winds blowing across the southern part of the city would waft "pestilential and disagreeable odors" from the immigrant center into their fine homes. Others feared that Europe's "riffraff" would congregate around the building. The *New York Daily Times* declared that the best solution would be to demolish the stone structure, arguing that it was a nuisance that blocked the harbor view from Battery Park.

The immigration commission promised that it would enclose the area with a fence as a barrier between the newcomers and the old neighborhood. They vowed that no persons would be housed overnight and that the area would not be used as a "victualling house" to serve food constantly. Physicians swore that subjecting immigrants to strict medical examinations was the best way to stop potential pestilence in the city. On June 8, 1855, the Superior Court lifted the temporary injunction.

The commission furiously set about converting the building from an entertainment palace to a workaday immigrant reception center. The seats were torn from the ground floor and replaced with functional wooden benches, creating space for 2,000 to 4,000 people. The once-fine "refreshment rooms" became public bathrooms, where constantly running water filled huge 20-foot bathtubs. Desks were created to process the immigrants, from entrance to departure by railroads. The place always would have an air of elegance, however crowded with immigrants; tall pillars still rose to support the roof high above the floor, and sunlight still streamed through the broad skylight.

On August 3, 1855, three ships debarked the first immigrants at Castle Garden, the forerunners of eight million foreigners who would enter America at the facility in the next 35 years. Incoming immigrants found the facility, while stricter than anything known before, also was more devoted to clearing the newcomers for entrance.

Commissioners boasted that immigrants could leave Castle Garden "without having their means impaired, their morals corrupted, and probably their persons diseased." By February 27, 1874, the *New York Times* could declare:

> Castle Garden is so well known in Europe that few emigrants can be induced to sail for any other destination. Their friends in this country write to those who are intending to emigrate to come to Castle Garden where they will be safe, and, if they are out of money, they can remain until it is sent to them. Complaints are frequently received by the commissioners from emigrants who have been landing at Halifax or Boston, though they were promised to be brought to New York. Thus emigrant runners abroad seek steerage passengers even by deception.

Castle Garden: the two words came to convey a new kind of welcome. In most European languages it was generally known by its correct name, but in a major exception, it also became "Kesselgardan" for large numbers of Europeans. Many immigrants who later came through Ellis Island after 1892 referred forever to what they thought had been a landing at vaunted Castle Garden.

As the result of a United States Senate inquiry into the causes and the extent of the "sickness and the mortality prevailing on the emigrant ships," newcomers sailing to New York were mildly helped by an Act of Congress adopted in March 1855 (before Castle Garden was opened). It called for larger and more sanitary individual sleeping quarters aboard immigrant ships and required each ship to produce a manifest containing the name of every passenger. The manifest had to be given on arrival in a debarking port to the customs collectors, who passed the record on to federal officials.

Such amenities did little for immigrants aboard the slow-moving, unkempt vessels that existed until the 1870s. Passengers constantly complained of poor food, rancid water, cramped sleeping quarters, rampaging epidemics of diseases, and the terror of steerage darkness during storms. In those days of sailing ships, a voyage from Great Britain to New York averaged about six weeks. The laws regarding food and space generally were ignored. The purpose of immigrants in the eyes of most skippers was to be a lucrative cash load. Sentiment was scant; it cost money.

One of the worst immigrant voyages ever recorded was on the sailing ship *Leibnitz*. It left Hamburg in late September 1867. Strong head winds forced the ship southward to the tropics, and the floundering vessel sailed for 14 weeks at the mercy of the gales and inept navigation before it crept into New York Harbor on January 11, 1868.

The boarding officer could scarcely believe his senses. He described the *Leibnitz* as the filthiest ship he had ever seen. The manifest showed that 108 of the original 544 passengers had died. Survivors told of corpses left in steerage for 24 hours or more, until vermin crept over them. The bodies then were cast into the sea. Horrified immigrant officials called the *Leibnitz* a "pesthole calculated to kill the healthiest man." With no doctor on board and the medical supplies gone after only two weeks, the ill-fated vessel became a floating chamber of horrors.

Although official records of fires at sea and ships that floundered and sank in wild storms are scant, there are instances of both. About a year before the opening of Castle Garden as an immigrant place of entry, the ship *Powhatan*, loaded with Germans bound for New York, sank in a wild storm off the New Jersey coast. The wreck took 354 lives and led, at least indirectly, to the formation of the first life saving service along the East Coast.

Most of the evils that beset immigrants escaped the attention of officials, both at European ports and at Castle Garden. New and broader immigrant policies were intended mainly to protect American cities and towns from the possibility that paupers and criminals would be dumped on their doorsteps. Additionally, there was an unwritten rule that "undesirables"—meaning non–Anglo-Saxons—must be discouraged from coming to America and barred whenever possible from entering.

Peter Morton Coan, a compiler of the opinions of Ellis Island immigrants, had this to say in the preface to his book *Ellis Island Interviews*:

> The purpose of Castle Garden, like Ellis Island after it, was to deny entrance to aliens deemed undesirable. This category included prostitutes, con men, Chinese "coolies," and "any convict, lunatic, idiot, or any person unable to take care of himself or herself without becoming a public charge."

Furthermore, immigration officials were unabashed in their preference for white northern Europeans. There is no known proof that this was written policy, but the attitude prevailed. "Politically correct" was not a concept in those days. Put another way, if you weren't white northern European and especially if you were black, Asian, or Hispanic, you were likely to be detained with an eye toward deportation.

Discomforts and inconveniences failed to stem or even slow the tide of aliens determined to share in the wealth—or supposed wealth—of America. In 1881, more than 455,600 immigrants landed at Castle Garden and successfully made their way through long lines and often confusing questions that had to be surmounted before the portals to freedom opened fully. In 1881, the incoming tide was even higher: 476,000, a high not to be matched again until 1903 at the Ellis Island facility.

About 70 percent of all the incoming foreigners arriving in the United States between 1855 and 1890 came through Castle Garden. The newcomers were mostly from Ireland, Germany, and England, although by the middle 1860s significant numbers of Swedes and other Scandinavian people joined the trek to America. The first known ship carrying Scandinavians, the sloop *Restauration*, left Stavanger in 1825, carrying 53 passengers to America. They were bound for western New York.

The opening of Castle Garden instituted a new and tougher (albeit safer and more equitable) period. Ships carrying immigrants first paused for quarantine at Staten Island, where doctors boarded the ship for a perfunctory examination of every passenger. Those who passed the quarantine examination (nearly all of them) continued their progress toward Castle Garden. Those who failed were sent to Ward's Island in the East River.

After Staten Island, ships proceeded northward through heavy traffic, ranging from barges to steam ferryboats to sailing ships, large and small. Ships carrying immigrants first docked at one of the numerous berths on the Hudson or East River. All passengers went through customs, then those in first class compartments went ashore without further examination. This would include any who were maimed or otherwise unlikely to pass a more rigorous examination at Castle Garden.

Steerage passengers trooped aboard barges for the short open-air trip to Castle Garden for an examination process that was scarcely unchanged through all the 35 years that it was the entering point for the incoming masses.

Each newcomer likely gasped with awe at the first sight of the interior of Castle Garden. Even with the decorations and ground level seats removed, the place was wondrously impressive with its high ceiling and its capacity to hold as many as 4,000 people.

The entering process was in retrospect startlingly simple, almost as if the people were Americans as soon as they had registered to sail from Europe. Physical examination was slight, more an eyeballing than a medical process. Inspectors sought to weed out those included among the wide categories of "undesirables." The building had a small hospital for persons who were ill with non-crippling sicknesses.

A definite idealism pervaded Castle Garden in its early days. At every turn there were staff employees capable of speaking several languages, a practice that might have seemed obvious considering the clientele but was reassuring to immigrants thrust into the shrillness of a virtual babel of conflicting tongues.

Once registered and accepted, an immigrant began to know the wonde
New World. Within Castle Garden he could exchange his native money for American dollars and cents, collect mail that might have been sent to him, write his own letters or send a telegram, and buy railroad tickets to nearly any destination in the United States.

A Labor Exchange opened at Castle Garden in 1868. It was both rewarding for the immigrants and of great use to employers who sought to hire some of the incoming foreigners. Previously the newcomers had been set loose to become the prey of self-appointed work peddlers outside the building. Only reputable requests for laborers, domestic servants, cooks, coal and iron miners, brick makers, and other unskilled jobs were accepted by the Labor Exchange.

The exchange tried to match the requests with people who had been classified by occupation soon after arrival. Laborers and farm workers could expect $6 to $10 a month plus room and board. Trained cooks received a bit more. The exchange sought wherever possible to keep families together. In the first year alone, 13,000 men and women were placed by the exchange without paying any fees or commissions.

No runners or outsiders were permitted near the immigrants within the center as they exchanged money or carried out other services to benefit themselves. Castle Garden officials were forbidden to suggest a certain route or railroad service in conflict with another. Church representatives or welfare agencies were permitted to help immigrants in such decisions. Inside the center, immigrants were in a cocoon of security.

A restaurant run as a contract amazed the newcomers. Prices were posted: beer, 10¢; coffee, 5¢; two-pound rye loaves, 10¢; a pound of bologna, 10¢; or a slice of pie at the same price. A large sandwich cost only 13¢. Signs urged customers to submit complaints or suggestions, something unheard of in their home countries (or for that matter, in nearly all restaurants or eating establishments in New York City).

The money-changing booth checked exchange rates three times daily and immediately posted the findings. A dozen railroads offered service—all in one convenient office. Baggage could be carried to uptown New York or to the New Jersey railroad stations for a set, non-negotiable price.

Harper's New Monthly Magazine sent a reporter to Castle Garden in 1871. His matter-of-fact report strengthened the notion that all was well at the immigrant center. Order and fairness seemed to be the order of the day:

> Slowly, one by one, the newcomers passed the two officers, whose duty it is to register every immigrant's name, birthplace and destinations in large

> folios. . . . On they passed, one by one, in single file till a few steps farther down they came to the desk of the so-called booker, a clerk of the Railway Association, whose duty it is to ascertain the destination of each passenger and furnish him with a printed slip, on which this is set forth, with the number of tickets wanted, and their cost in currency.

If all of that seemed idyllic, it was, particularly in the first years. It would not last, as will be described later. But the early order and honor in handling immigrants was not a textbook proscribing. It was a new experiment in handling huge—and not necessarily well-liked—crowds in a radically different environment.

Outside the Garden, it was every man for himself. One report told of the reaction of an Irish immigrant who had safely weathered the storm of Liverpool's crooks, swindlers, cheats, and sharpsters as he strode along the docks to board a ship for America. The Irishman found much the same conditions on the streets outside Castle Garden: "People may think that if they get safe through Liverpool they are all right, but I can assure you that there is greater robberies done in New York on immigrants than there is in Liverpool."

Boarding houses for those uncertain of their ultimate location in America abounded near Castle Garden. They were licensed by the Immigration Commissioners for $25 and were regularly inspected, although the inspections tended to be cursory. One boarding house owner testified before a congressional committee that his place had two sitting rooms, a dining room, and sleeping quarters for 100 people. He exchanged money and ran a bar, which he said operated mainly to sell postage stamps.

Eventually eyebrows would be raised and indignation would be stirred by such peculiar testimony, but for a brief shining time, decency prevailed at Castle Garden. Immigrants could—and did—write home of the wonders of New York Harbor and the bustling port city.

The numbers of immigrants dropped sharply during the Civil War. Simultaneously, thousands of young Irish and German sons of immigrants in New York City and surrounding areas hastened to join the Union Army. The United States of America had become their land and the Union was their cause. People in the North set aside prejudices to welcome immigrant enlistments. By 1870, however, the pace of immigration began a sharp rise in number—and in the negative feelings toward the European aliens.

America came of age in the Civil War and by 1870 the 37 states were linked by a telegraph system and a transcontinental railroad. Alaska, twice the size of Texas, had been purchased in 1867 and the entire western frontier of the contiguous United States was being opened to settlement and exploitation. Inventors, led by Thomas Edison, were transforming the nation. Industrial giants were rising, in steel, in railroads, in petroleum, in sugar, in coal, in communications, in textiles, in lumber, and in dozens more mushrooming enterprises. The sprawling lands of the West were becoming developed. The nation desperately needed a great army of new workers. Europe was ready to supply them.

A widely-distributed 1870 lithograph captured what the immigrants saw as their vessels slowly moved through teeming New York Harbor. Hundreds of vessels of all sizes, shapes, and types dominated the scene. Two-, three-, four-, and even five-masted sailing ships moved slowly through the scene or lay at anchor just off Castle Garden. Bossy little steam-powered tugs swirled in and out of the slow-moving traffic, giving wide berth to the huge, clumsy barges floating downstream. Several steam-powered side-wheelers could be seen, on their way to Albany or toward destinations up the East River to Long Island Sound.

Most of the immigrants left New York by train, either northward from the city or increasingly on emigrant trains that steamed out of New Jersey stations in Jersey City, Hoboken, or Weehawken. The new Americans waited on open platforms, burned by summer's sun and whipped by winter's winds, before boarding rundown passenger cars consigned to the immigrant service.

Immigrant trains operated on the loosest of schedules, or, too often, on no schedule at all. There were few amenities. Sleeping cars or dining cars for immigrants would have been considered laughable. Departures were irregular; railroad companies had only modest interest in foreigners beyond collecting their ticket money. The trains rolled toward Pennsylvania's coal mining towns, onward to the Great Lake ports, still onward into territories on the verge of becoming states, and by 1880 immigrants could entrain for the fabulous open lands that railroads made available in California for pittances.

In the final decade (1880–1890) of Castle Garden's function as an immigration center, of the 5,500,000 immigrants who came to America, more than 3,780,000 of them entered via Castle Garden. By 1885 it became all too clear that the aging center could not possibly continue to handle the successive waves of newcomers.

The federal government openly proclaimed that immigrants had become a major problem, not because of who they were or the way they behaved but because of the lack of federal interest and little or no federal regulation. On August 3, 1882, the government finally enacted the first comprehensive national immigrant law, the Act to Regulate Immigration.

There is no question that the new law was prompted as much, or perhaps more, by fears of "undesirables" entering America than any compassion for the poverty-stricken newcomers streaming down the gangplanks. Attitudes about the "new breed" of immigrants grew increasingly truculent; in 1882 Congress also passed a law barring Chinese from entering the country, chiefly, it was said, because of low wage rates accepted by Oriental workers.

Three years later, labor union pressure prompted the federal government to prevent business and industrial leaders from contracting and importing gangs of male immigrants who would work for wages far under the rates that labor had won after years of strife. Federal agents who came to Castle Garden were there to enforce the new law strictly.

Under the national legislation of 1882, each state that admitted aliens had to appoint state-run boards to inspect immigrants under regulations that were the same in all ports. The principal concern was to turn back those thought to be unworthy. Shipping lines were required to pay 50¢ per immigrant to help defray the costs of administering landing depots and hospitals. The New York Board of Commissioners quickly agreed to the legislation—and set about continuing what it had essentially been doing since 1855, without the 50¢ admission levy.

The old idealism slipped away. By 1880 complaints were rife about the handling of immigrants at Castle Garden; some were inspired by business or political foes. But enough were real enough to cause mounting concern. Charges ranged from political patronage to excessive charges for railroad tickets, from charges of abusive treatment of men and women to accounts of sexual misbehavior, including rape.

Pressure to clean up Castle Garden's situation picked up pace. In 1883, New York Governor Grover Cleveland spoke (many among the employees thought unfairly) about "unblushing peculation" at Castle Garden. He was blunt when he declared that "the present management of this very important department is a scandal and a reproach to civilization." It would take seven more years for Castle Garden to collapse, but Cleveland's bitter words were in essence the valedictory of the immigration depot.

Labor unions especially chafed constantly at the practice of labor suppliers who visited European countries, ignoring the law, to sign potential workers to work contracts that would bind them to an employer when they entered America.

Incensed by reports of swindling and immorality within Castle Garden, Joseph Pulitzer, editor of the prestigious *New York World*, led city newspapers in demanding changes. On July 27, 1887, in an editorial titled "Castle Garden's Monopoly: Cogent Reasons for the Abolition of the Emigration Commission," he railed against what he believed to be the restriction of competition among railroad lines for immigrant passengers:

> It [Castle Garden] was organized in order that the hundreds of thousands of immigrants that come to these shores every year might be protected and cared for until they reached their destination; but instead of doing this, the commission throws the immigrants into the hands of a heartless railroad pool that treats them most shamefully and squeezes all it can out of them.
>
> The immigrants are not only huddled like cattle in the uncomfortable and foul-smelling cars of this unlawful pool, that run on a freight schedule, taking two days instead of one to reach Chicago, but they are deprived of the right to select by which one of the pool lines they shall purchase tickets, and are charged exorbitant rates for baggage.

Pulitzer's empathy for immigrant problems was not a passing thing. Born in Hungary in 1847, he was an immigrant himself, having come to America in 1864 when a recruiter signed him to fight for the Union Army. He entered the United States through Castle Garden. After a post-war career that ranged from laborer to newspaper editor, he bought the foundering *New York World* in 1878 and turned it into a vigorous, crusading paper than won him both fame and fortune.

Washington finally called up the heavy artillery of investigation in the summer of 1887 when the secretary of the treasury authorized a study of immigration. A year later, the Senate and House of Representatives both appointed committees to investigate the volatile (but politically self-serving) issue of immigration.

No one was startled by the findings: that Castle Garden's space and location were pitifully inadequate for the daily flow of immigrants, that newcomers were being fleeced on site by the railroads and money changers, that immigrants were being abused and mistreated, and, from a political standpoint, worst of all, "large numbers of persons not lawfully entitled to land in the United States are annually received at this port."

The capstone came from a member of the New York state commissioner of immigration. He told a committee of the House of Representatives that Castle Garden was "a perfect farce." The time had come for the federal government to assume complete responsibility for immigration.

Despite the intense criticism in its dying days, Castle Garden had served reasonably well. In its 45 years of existence, it admitted and processed 7.5 million newcomers to America, initially mainly from Ireland and Germany but later in an emerging flood of immigrants from southern and eastern Europe.

ELLIS ISLAND

The 1890 Census was a splendid tool for measuring immigration. Under the listing "foreign origins" it counted 20,645,542 residents of the United States who were either immigrants or the children of at least one immigrant parent. They were mainly from northern Europe's so-called Anglo-Saxon nations.

In February of 1890, the United States notified the New York commissioners who ran Castle Garden that the federal government would assume full jurisdiction for people entering the United States, starting on April 18, 1890. That day, Castle Garden's gangplanks would be drawn up, ending 45 years of immigrants streaming through the aging facility.

On closing day, two ships, the steamers *Bohemia* and *State of Indiana*, discharged a total of 465 immigrants at Castle Garden. The doors closed behind them. The search for a new location, preferably in the open harbor on an available island, necessarily proceeded at a brisk pace: the New York commissioners, angered by the precipitate action of Congress, refused further rental of Castle Garden by the federal government.

Attention centered on three islands in the New York harbor—Governor's Island, a very short ferry ride to The Battery, and Bedloe's Island and Ellis Island, both close to the New Jersey mainland and both about 2 miles southwest of New York City. Immigration to America was about to take a formidable turn.

After six years of darkness and neglect, Castle Garden reopened as a municipal aquarium in 1897. Opening day attracted 30,000 people eager to see the splendors of aquatic life. Many millions of visitors came in the next 45 years, until the aquarium was closed (but not demolished) in 1940 to make room for the Brooklyn-Battery Tunnel. The aquarium soon was moved to Coney Island, and in 1950 the old fort was declared a national monument.

Chapter Four

"GIVE ME YOUR TIRED, YOUR POOR"

Michigan Congressman Melbourne Ford, whose scathing report on conditions at Castle Garden in 1888 had been the death blow to the aging complex, insisted that any new immigration depot must be in New York Harbor. His choice was one of the Oyster Islands close to the New Jersey mainland. The name derived from the oysters that once were plucked from the mud flats surrounding the little islands.

There were two prominent Oyster Island sites: Ellis Island and Bedloe's Island. Ford chose Bedloe's. Unfortunately for the congressman, Bedloe's Island already had a tenant, a 151-foot-tall lady whose shining torch dominated the harbor. She was the Statue of Liberty, dedicated in 1886. That might not have meant much in Michigan in 1890, but in New York it was tantamount to asking the city to assassinate its most favored and most beloved personage. The statue's popularity was strange and sudden, for as late as 1884 the city did not even want her in the harbor.

New York's spectacular lady had been conceived in Paris in 1865, as the notion of Edouard Rene de Laboulaye, a leading French legal scholar. At a dinner party attended by sculptor Frederic Auguste Bartholdi, Laboulaye suggested that France cement its friendship with America by building a monument in Paris that would be presented to the United States as a symbol of French assistance to America during the Revolutionary War.

Bartholdi visited the United States in late May 1871. As his ship sailed slowly through The Narrows, his eyes dwelled on the great clusters of long, low buildings, topped by the Trinity Church spire. Then Bartholdi saw Bedloe's Island, only a few hundred feet east of the booming Central Railroad of New Jersey yards. The stone walls of old, abandoned Fort Wood, long a Bedloe's Island fixture, rose above the tides. Bartholdi later recalled his vision: "When I first saw Bedloe's Island, I suddenly realized what the statue would look like and where it would stand—right on the island, against the sky, welcoming all people coming to America."

He then traveled westward across the nation by train—to Niagara Falls, Chicago, across the western plains, and over the Rocky Mountains to Salt Lake City, then on to San Francisco. It was a remarkable trip, especially considering that the transcontinental railroad had been finished only two years before. Bartholdi knew far more about the vast size and the magnificent complexity of the United States than all but a handful of the nation's citizens.

Bartholdi certainly sensed that Americans were cool to the notion of a statue in New York Harbor, even if France were to build it without cost. Undeterred, Bartholdi pressed on. He sculpted his first version of his statue, which he named La Liberte Eclairant Le Monde (Liberty Enlightening the World). In her first incarnation, she was 1.25 meters (about 4 feet) tall.

Modifications came slowly. Bartholdi shifted Liberty's torch from her left hand to her right and placed a tablet of laws in her bent left arm. He put shackles on her ankles and gave her a seven-pointed crown to represent the seven continents and the seven seas. She was beautiful. In his final plan, her tall, vigorously-striding body resembled that of the sculptor's mistress, Jean-Emilie Baheux de Puysieux, a dressmaker's assistant. (She later became his wife.) The face resembled Bartholdi's stern-willed mother, Auguste-Charlotte Bartholdi, whose opinion of her son's mistress can only be imagined.

Thrice enlarged, the model finally stood 151 feet tall, her ultimate height. Each enlargement required more than 9,000 modifications and corrections of distortions. As he worked on the enlargements, Bartholdi decided that the towering lady must be fashioned from sheets of gleaming copper, light enough to make it feasible to ship the panels to America.

Bartholdi had hoped to deliver the Statue of Liberty intact on July 4, 1876, the 100th anniversary of the first public reading of the Declaration of Independence. A 30-foot high arm and torch arrived in late August for display at the Philadelphia Centennial Exposition. Another two years passed before the head with its crown of seven spears was put on display at the Paris Exposition of 1878.

The totally aborted time schedule was disturbing. Americans were showing a strange indifference to the emerging statue. When Bartholdi visited America again to attend the Centennial Exposition, he was most often received with indifference or outright rudeness. The American government refused to grant any money and big business merely yawned at the thought of financing a pedestal for a statue on Bedloe's Island.

Bartholdi's lowest emotional point came on September 29, 1876, when a bitter *New York Times* editorial ridiculed the statue and charged that the French public had raised $200,000 only to have it squandered by the sculptor with nothing to show but an arm and a torch. The *Times* writer felt that the huge arm (and the overall concept of the statue) were ridiculous. He sought a laugh: "The thumbnail affords an easy seat for the largest fat woman now in existence."

Continuing the sarcastic tone, the *Times*'s editorial writer poured on the venom. Why send an arm, he asked? Why not send a foot, a calf, a knee, with each dedicated as it was added to a rising statue? Eventually, the head would be attached and there would stand Bartholdi's lady.

The *Times* erred grievously when it stated that the United States would be stuck for $1.8 million to complete the statue. It had been clear from the start that France would pay for the statue and that the United States would erect the pedestal on which it would stand. The *Times* version was a blatant lie. The paper was not yet the great, truth-seeking journalistic icon that it would become. The ineffective libel laws of the day left no room for legal action.

Tired and sick at heart, Bartholdi fled New York and headed for Newport, Rhode Island, to visit an artist friend. Jeanne-Emilie, the sculptor's mistress, now living in Canada, journeyed southward and the two were married on December 20, 1876, far from the frowning presence of Bartholdi's mother. They sailed for home, to tell her of the marriage and to permit work on the statue to pick up pace.

Bartholdi ordered 200,000 pounds of the copper plates, each about the thickness of a modern quarter-dollar coin. It is important to know that the statue is an astounding assemblage of parts, each designed so that the total would be light enough to transport to America.

The statue was divided into 200 pieces of varying sizes; each was fashioned on one of Bartholdi's 200 wooden molds, against which the plates were hammered into shape. The work was doubly difficult because the hammering was against reverse molds, meaning that the individual plates were made inside out.

The project outgrew Bartholdi's original studio. He moved into a new space and increased his work force to 20 artisans. His "liberty factory" became the center of organized chaos for nearly six years—an arm here, pieces of the head and face there; here some toes, there a sandal; here the intricate fold of a skirt, there a segment of the crown.

Any stranger who looked into Bartholdi's studio-factory between 1876 and 1881 could have been excused for believing that he had happened on an eerie gargantuan house of body parts:

A long aquiline nose, 4 feet, 6 inches long, stood taller than a ten-year-old boy or girl.

Five or six adults could stand on Miss Liberty's hand, 16 feet, 5 inches long from wrist to a fingernail's tip.

An index finger was 8 feet long, an eye 2 1/2 feet across, her mouth 3 feet wide.

The right arm, the one that would hold the torch, was 42 feet long, taller than a three-story house.

Good news and bad news flooded in on Bartholdi. On the good side, the United States Congress unanimously accepted the French gift of the statue on February 22, 1877. The bad news was perhaps anticipated: Congress failed to appropriate any money for the statue or its erection in New York.

A major worry plagued Bartholdi: how could he insure that the statue would remain standing in the high winds that often buffeted The Narrows? In 1879 he turned to Gustav Eiffel, the leading young engineer in Paris. Eiffel's reputation at the time depended on dazzling bridges he had built in several European cities. His great triumph, to be known as "Eiffel's Tower" was still in the future.

Eiffel designed the "skeleton" on which the copper plates would be securely hung. With that concern out of the way, Bartholdi could rejoice in the flood of money pouring in from the people of France. Contributions came from a nationwide lottery, the sale of small replicas of the proposed statue, and small contributions from 100,000 French citizens. By 1879, more than $250,000 had been subscribed (none of it from the French government).

With no assurance that America would provide the pedestal for Miss Liberty, Bartholdi decided to erect her in the streets of Paris. On October 24, 1881, on the 100th anniversary of the American victory at Yorktown (which was made possible by French aid), Levi P. Morton, American ambassador to France, accepted the statue for America.

By July 4, 1884, the gleaming statue rose high above the rooftops of Paris. That day she passed from being an adopted daughter of France to the spurned daughter of America. Miss Liberty had come of age. France's most famous emigrant was ready to cross the ocean to her new home, provided that America showed evidence that it really wanted her.

Money trickled in to the American committee for the pedestal. Working on faith, the committee broke ground for the pedestal in the late winter of 1883. Workers excavated a huge, square pit on Bedloe's Island, into which they poured an enormous tapering block of concrete—53 feet deep, 91 feet square at the bottom, and 65 feet square at the top. It was the largest concrete mass in the world at the time.

On August 5, 1884, when the pedestal's cornerstone was laid, thunder and lightning riveted the skies and heavy rain poured down throughout the ceremony. It was the prophecy of doom. A few weeks later, all work ceased. The committee had raised $182,491.40 and had spent $179,624.51—leaving a balance of $2,866.89. At least $125,000 more was needed.

Cartoonists and critics had a field day. Miss Liberty was shown as a decrepit old hag, begging on the streets for money to finish the pedestal. If anyone in government or business cared, there was no rush of income.

As New York City stalled, offers to welcome Miss Liberty poured into France from other American cities, including Philadelphia, Boston, Cleveland, and even distant San Francisco. The American committee warned in a widely-distributed and plaintive pamphlet that the statue might go elsewhere. The committee said, "Citizens of the state, citizens of the metropolis, we ask you once and for all to prevent so painful and so humiliating a catastrophe."

Joseph Pulitzer, crusading editor of the *New York World*, leaped into the chasm of despair. Pulitzer needed a cause to help build the lagging circulation of his newspaper An immigrant himself, he enthusiastically attacked the money problem.

Pulitzer became passionate about the need for "little people" to join him in building the pedestal. He told of the statue: "paid for in France by working men, tradesmen, shop girls, artisans all, irrespective of class or condition, standing pathetically on the streets of Paris." He exaggerated some; funds for the statue had also come from some wealthy French donors.

Pulitzer was on a crusade. He pleaded for money, in any amount, promising that every donation would be acknowledged in the *World*. The pennies, nickels, and dimes rolled in, from New York street urchins, from distant hamlets and cities, from school children, from orphanages, and from gifts such as the two pet bantams that Florence de Forest of Metuchen, New Jersey, sent in to be sold with the proceeds going to the fund. A few wealthy donors such as Pierre Lorrillard, the tobacco entrepreneur, sent moderate contributions.

The *New York Times* initially gave indirect endorsement to the fund. On June 23, 1885 the *Times* sent $250 to the *World* and promised full support. An editorial in the *Times* was warm and gracious in praise: "It is not easy to see what might have been done with M. Bartholdi's colossal statue if the *World* had not labored with such zeal and persistence to provide a standing place for it."

Pulitzer delivered the funds in segments, finally finishing the task on August 11,1885, when he handed the committee the last payment of $192,006.39. Pulitzer cherished the last 39 cents. His campaign had been all about pennies, and he printed the name of every donor, down to donations of 1¢.

Paris grieved as the towering lady was slowly dismantled for shipment to America. Each copper segment was numbered and all abutting pieces were identified with matching marks. The skeleton and frame parts were packed into 14 crates, of many sizes and shapes, ranging in weight from 150 pounds to 3 tons.

The crates were loaded aboard 70 railroad freight cars and taken to the river port at Rouen and loaded aboard the ship *Isere*. The precious cargo left France on May 22, 1885, and entered New York Harbor 26 days later, on June 17.

The French North Atlantic Squadron met the freighter at Sandy Hook and escorted her into The Narrows. There, 90 American ships—both the U.S. Navy and private vessels—joined the parade that the *Times* called "the most brilliant pageant ever in American waters." The hills along The Narrows were "black with spectators."

The *Isere* tied up at Bedloe's Island. The crates were taken ashore to await completion of the pedestal, which was finished in April 1885. Two months later Eiffel's skeleton loomed against the sky, the "bones" of its right arm thrust high. Fastening the plates to the skeleton began on July 11, when the first of 600,000 copper rivets was driven into place.

President Grover Cleveland arrived by train from Washington on October 27 to be prepared for the dedication of the statue the next day. A vast throng had slept on the streets along the parade route. They awakened on Dedication Day, drenched by the pouring, cold rain.

President Cleveland and about 4,000 special invited guests boarded chartered ferryboats and rode to Bedloe's Island through the driving rain and lowering fog. Bartholdi had been on the island for several hours and had climbed the 168 inside steps to the crown. His role in the ceremony would be surprisingly small: he would await a signal (a little boy waving a white handkerchief) to proclaim that the main speaker had finished. Bartholdi would then unveil Miss Liberty's face.

William Evarts, one of the most popular (and most long winded) speakers of the day rose to begin his address as the darkness began to deepen. He paused after five or six sentences to wipe his brow. The signal boy, an unknown hero in light of Evarts's penchant for long-lasting oratory, mistook the speaker's long pause to be the end of the talk.

The boy raised his handkerchief. Peering through the gloom, Bartholdi thought it was the signal. He undid the veil covering the statue's head; it dropped and Miss Liberty's face shone forth.

The harbor erupted in tumultuous noise. Naval guns fired roaring salutes. Shrill boat whistles cut through the fog. Fireworks exploded on shore and hundreds of thousands of voices rose in a thundering roar of welcome. Up in the statue, high above the excitement, Bartholdi wept.

President Cleveland delivered the final words of welcome, in words of warmth that ring eternally:

> We will not forget that Liberty has made this her home. Nor shall her chosen altar be neglected. Willing votaries will constantly keep alive its fires and these shall gleam upon the shores of our sister republic in the East. Reflecting these and joined with answering rays, a stream of light shall pierce the darkness of ignorance and man's oppression until Liberty enlightens the world.

Miss Liberty, the greatest immigrant of them all, was home. She was about to become a woman of the world.

The Statue of Liberty was not conceived and sculpted as a symbol of immigration, but it quickly became so as immigrant ships passed under the torch and the shining face, heading toward Ellis Island. However, it was a poem written in 1883 that permanently stamped on Miss Liberty the role of unofficial greeter of incoming immigrants. When Emma Lazarus, an immigrant herself, penned the words, she could not have seen the statue, although she might have seen or read about the giant lady then almost completed on the streets of Paris. Her powerful words were provoked by the terrible massacres of Jews in Russia. Her poem is inscribed on a bronze plaque that was placed near the base of the pedestal in 1903:

> Not like the brazen giant of Greek fame,
> With conquering limbs astride from land to land;
> Here at our sea-washed, sunset gates shall stand
> A mighty woman with a torch, whose flame
> Is the imprisoned lightning, and her name
> Mother of Exiles. From her beacon-hand
> Glows world-wide welcome; her mild eyes command
> The air-bridged harbors that twin cities frame.
> "Keep ancient lands, your storied pomp!" cries she
> With silent lips. "Give me your tired, your poor
> Your huddled masses yearning to breath free.
> The wretched refuse of your teeming shore.
> Send these, the homeless, tempest-tosst to me,
> I lift my lamp beside the golden door!"

Chapter Five

INVITATIONS TO THE LAND OF GOLD

America changed dramatically after 1860. Northern factories that had expanded to arm and supply Union forces presaged the age of huge factories and ever-increasing work forces. Old-time enterprises, such as ships, lumber, bricks, and iron products, found increased demand. Inventors perfected typewriters, linotype machines, safety bicycles, new kinds of synthetic products, molding machines, the telephone, the electric light, the phonograph, and hundreds of other instruments or processes certain to change America's way of life.

The iron mines of New Jersey and the coal mines of Pennsylvania and West Virginia expanded to meet surging demands. Railroads hastened the double tracking of their lines and the elevation of rights-of-way through cities. The popularity of brick in factory construction revitalized brick yards. Textile manufacture and factory-made clothing become major industries. A rage for paper after the Civil War forced paper factories to expand.

Two New Jersey factories erected in 1873 illustrate the fabulous size of new factories. Each was created to meet demands for new products—sewing machines in one case, a new synthetic substance called Celluloid in the other.

Isaac Singer, whose name will always be linked around the world with sewing machines, consolidated several factories into one huge building in Elizabethport, New Jersey, in 1873 at a cost of $3 million, an enormous sum for that period. He hired 3,000 employees to run the sprawling modern factory, a model for ensuing construction. Thousands, then millions, of the compact Singer sewing machines went outward, many of them into the homes of immigrants slaving at piecework in their New York City flats.

Celluloid was essentially an accidental discovery. Experimenting in his landlady's kitchen in Albany, New York, in quest of a substance to replace ivory in billiard balls, John Wesley Hyatt mixed pyroxylin (highly explosive nitroglycerin) with camphor. The result was a synthetic that hardened into a moldable substance called Celluloid. It quickly became useful in making items that ranged from harness ornaments to dolls, combs, and brush handles, and eventually celluloid collars and cuffs. Hyatt moved into a five-story factory in Newark, New Jersey in 1873 and hired thousands of workers.

Those were but two examples of the growth of factories in America. Each was a new idea rather than an expansion of manufacturing an old product. Each had machines that could be run by unskilled workers or a product that could be made by untrained labor. The new source of such unskilled manpower had to come from Europe, particularly from the nations of southern and eastern Europe.

Yet of all the lures cast before European immigrants, none was greater than the wiles used by transatlantic steamship companies and American railroads. The United States government was an unwitting conspirator with the railroads. As a spur to the building railroads west of the Mississippi River, Congress allocated land for each mile of track in place. Grants were for 10 to 20 miles of land on both sides of the railroad, for the full distance that the line traversed.

By 1865, railroad entrepreneurs had been granted 184 million acres of western land. Unless it could be settled or exchanged for other favors, their vast acreage throughout western states and territories might as well have been desert sand dunes. Immigrants were obvious targets for cheap land. They would, as well, pay fares to reach the distant property.

In one of the great coincidences in world history, at the same time that America needed them, the numbers of Europeans willing to leave home intensified. Vincent N. Parillo, in his book *Strangers to the Shores*, provided a concise summary of merging conditions that made southern and eastern Europeans eager to flee their homelands:

> Peasant life was especially harsh in Europe. The ruling classes and local estate farm owners ruthlessly exploited the common people. They crushed most peasant revolts and protests instead of reforming the basic agricultural economy. Peasants saw their sons drafted into the army for periods of 12 to 31 years. Trying to eke out an existence amid poverty, unemployment, sickness, and tyranny, many of Europe's poor looked elsewhere for a better life. . . .
>
> Political and economic unrest in Europe also encouraged the exodus. Old World governments faced pressures of overpopulation, chronic poverty, the decline of feudalism, dissident factions, and a changing agrarian economy. For them, large scale emigration to the United States provided an expedient means of easing societal pressures without actually addressing the root causes of many institutional problems, so they [governments] sponsored emigrant drives, further increasing the European migration.

ELLIS ISLAND

Cartoons and editorials in American newspapers pictured foreign newcomers pushing their way into America as an overwhelming and unwanted horde, boldly usurping privileges and threatening to steal jobs from "native" Americans, most of whom had long forgotten their own immigrant roots. Uncle Sam was depicted as the besieged symbol of Americanism.

Even Woodrow Wilson, president of Princeton University and a highly respected national scholar, took umbrage at the immigrants who were arriving in America after 1890. He wrote in his massive five-volume *A History of the American People*, published in 1901, a damning indictment of the "new" immigrants who were arriving from southern and eastern Europe:

> Immigrants poured steadily in as before, but with an alteration of stock which students of affairs marked with uneasiness. Throughout the century men of the sturdy stocks of the north of Europe had made up the main stream of foreign blood which every year added to the vital working force of the country.
>
> But now there came multitudes of men of the lowest class from the south of Italy and men of the meaner sort out of Hungary and Poland, men of the ranks where there was neither skill nor energy nor any initiative of quick intelligence; and they came in numbers which increased from year, as if the countries of the south of Europe were disburdening themselves of the more hapless elements of their population, the men whose standards of life and of work were such as American workmen had never dreamed of hitherto.

The austere, aristocratic Ivy League president almost surely had never worked with or probably never even met such an immigrant in his elegant ivory tower, but he echoed the kind of 1890s social judgments being heaped on immigrants from the castles of industry, the halls of organized labor, the carefully-exclusive country clubs, the haunts of self-appointed "high society," and even in many Protestant churches where ministers expressed unabashed hatred of the "new" immigrants in general and of Roman Catholics in particular.

Despite such prejudices, as the nineteenth century entered its last decades the United States desperately and constantly needed new workers. Immigrants had been invited and pressured to come to America since the 1820s, coaxed by promises of golden streets, infinite opportunities, unlimited cheap land, and immediate work at good wages.

Invitations to the Land of Gold

America initially needed immigrant muscle to extend railroads and canals across the vast territory between the Atlantic and Pacific Oceans. But with the rising of huge new factories and a surge of inventions creating new products, the nation had an unparalleled demand for unskilled workers. Nouveau riche millionaires moving into suburbs that ringed New York City pleaded for laborers to landscape their properties and to work inside their mansions. Booming Pennsylvania coal mines and New Jersey iron mines required ever more bodies to labor in the pits.

"Come to America" invitations spread across Europe like a paper hurricane created by industries, shipping companies, railroads, and individual states, all willing to use any verbal subterfuges, exaggerations, and outright lies to entice immigrants to leave for Ellis Island. If that weren't enough, immigrants who had gone to America before wrote home, urging family members or former neighbors to join them on the golden streets of America.

Europe was saturated with news and information about America in the 1840s. Immigrant officials recognized that many immigrants knew more about the United States, particularly the just-opened territories, than most Americans. Many immigrants arrived with maps, folders, or even books describing the New World and its opportunities.

Guide books were written by agencies promoting emigration, and thus were filled with descriptions of favored steamship lines with steerage accommodations or railroad connections in America. One particularly favored book, *Where to Emigrate and Why*, published by Americus in 1869, told of ships headed for America with connections to transportation in the new land, as well as potential jobs and wages.

States and cities vied for immigrants. New Jersey Governor George B. McClellan's annual message in 1879 urged that New Jersey's soil, taxes, climate, and nearness to good markets be brought to the notice of immigrants. An official State of New Jersey broadside enhanced the invitation in 1880:

> Why should the immigrant go to Minnesota, where the climate is like Sweden, when he can secure a home in the southern part of New Jersey, where the climate is more like the southern part of France or the shores of the Mediterranean?

The rest of the broadside was so lavish in praise of the state, particularly its southern agricultural opportunities, that it is a wonder that newcomers went anywhere else. The appeal was obviously directed at Italians, many of whom already had become vegetable and fruit growers in Vineland, a New Jersey town founded in

1861 on the principle that educated New Englanders would comprise an inner town, surrounded by immigrant farmers.

That same year of 1880 brought a glowing counter proposal from then little-settled Missouri. Its brochure included railroad and steamship advice, as well as information on property that could be had for less than $300 for a 40-acre farm. The climate was said to be: ". . . a golden mean between the extremes of cold in the north and the heat of the south, thus rendering its temperature highly adapted to promote the prolific principle in man and nature."

California, already well known abroad because of the gold rush in 1849, tied its appeals to the Union Pacific Railroad, the transcontinental route completed in 1869. Aided by the railroad, which had hundreds of thousands of acres of land to sell, the State of California sent posters and billboards to Europe to proclaim the far western state as "The Cornucopia of the World," where (according to the poster) 43,795,000 acres of "government lands" were available.

California and the Union Pacific, like most western states and western railroads, desperately needed people to buy land, to work it, and to work on and ride the railroads. When the need for workers decreased, the railroads stepped up their quest for ticket-buying passengers.

California's cornucopia was featured on European billboards lauding the Pacific Ocean state from thousands of walls, wooden fences, and railroad stations throughout Europe. Its colorful cornucopia told of available land that was of course healthful, with a "climate for health and wealth without cyclones or blizzards." According to the Golden State's promoters, "a million farmers" could be accommodated.

Other railroads west of the Mississippi River acquired millions of acres of land when they extended tracks across the plains and through Rocky Mountain passes. Much of that land was nearly worthless from an economic standpoint and it would stay that way unless the railroads could sell the acreage. The best propects in the world seemed to be immigrants, if they could be persuaded that all anyone needed in order to buy land was a small down payment. The Union Pacific, for example, advertised on European billboards that it owned or controlled 12 million acres of open land, "located in the great central belt of population, commerce and wealth, and adjoining the world's highway [the railroad] from ocean to ocean."

The Union Pacific had intense competitors. The Central Pacific advertised "immigrant tickets at low rates" on "daily trains from Boston, New York, Philadelphia, Baltimore, Chicago, St. Louis, Omaha and intermediate points, for San Francisco." The Burlington & Missouri River Railroad proclaimed throughout

Europe that it had Iowa and Nebraska lands for sale "on ten years credit." It offered tickets from New York for "land exploring."

Scotland's Glasgow and Southwestern Railway Company circulated posters for its "through tickets to Kansas, Nebraska and Colorado. In the United States of America." Its trains connected with steamship lines in Liverpool. From there, if the railroad could be believed, it was merely an ocean cruise and a comfortable railroad trip to beyond the Mississippi River.

One of the steamship lines in Liverpool was the White Star Line, whose broadsides made steerage seem almost ideal. Individual adult fares were six pounds and six shillings (about $30), "including a plentiful supply of cooked provisions." Children under eight years were half fare and infant tickets cost one pound, one shilling. White Star told billboard readers that its accommodations were "of the very highest character—good food, individual berths, families berthed together and other amenities."

Railroad agents, steamship company representatives, and American land agents could be found in every major European city or town. They competed vigorously for passengers, almost always describing considerably more than an immigrant might really hope to get on a railroad, a steamship, or from a land purchase. But the travel terms were understandable, reasonable in price, and offered the potential excitement of an ocean voyage. There also was little question that life in America had a greater present and a more promising future than nearly all parts of Europe.

By 1897, large numbers of Americans looked on the "New Immigrants"—poverty stricken Italians, persecuted Russian Jews, the Poles, the Hungarians, the Slovakians—as a social and economic evil. They were deemed pushy foreigners, clustering together in hovels, speaking strange tongues, eating strange foods—and taking jobs from "good Americans," all of whom were themselves immigrants or were descended from those who had paved the way into the United States.

The United States was exploding in all directions, in factory output, in new estates, in inventions. It needed bodies of all sizes to do the roughest of manual labor and the most delicate of household chores, from kitchen work to maid service. Railroads had land to sell. Steamship companies had space to sell on their liners. Out went the welcoming word to villages and cities in Europe: Come to America!

It is important to stress that these "pushy" foreigners with the strange modes of speech and exotic appetites were invited to come to America. Those billboards and signs and ticket offices were not figments of the imagination. Their messages were as real as wartime posters: We need YOU! They were invitations to wallow in the great spree of prosperity mushrooming across the United States.

None of the messages of welcome said anything about the menial jobs, the city slums, the American scorn that would be heaped on the heads of newcomers. Certainly no letter writer would talk of the ugly, insulting nicknames hurled at immigrants. None talked about the sickening dangers in the mine pits and in the flapping belts and rapidly moving machines in city factories.

The tidal wave of southern and eastern Europeans responding to the many and varied invitations is best demonstrated in raw figures. In 1854, on the eve of the opening of Castle Garden, Anglo-Saxon immigrants represented 85 to 90 percent of all those who entered America. In 1872, only about 10 percent were southern or eastern Europeans. By 1907, about three quarters of immigrants came from Russia, Italy, Austria-Hungary, the Balkans, and Greece.

Uniting all of the efforts from abroad were the letters sent home by relatives or friends already in America and the occasional visitor who had returned from America to bring his family to the United States, to find a wife, or just to show off how good America had been to him.

Few individual letters have survived, but the newspapers of Italy, Greece, Slovakia, and other places often printed letters from America. Nearly all of them were upbeat; who would admit that the trials of getting to America were not worth the while? Who would say that prosperity was not the norm? Who would not urge others to join them?

In 1896 a Swede wrote home from Knoxville, Illinois, hewing to the prosaic theme that "the soil here is good and fruitful." Another Swede wrote home at about the same time, declaring, "I had planned last Christmas that I would spend this Christmas in Sweden—but when I gave more thought to the matter, what can one do in Sweden but work for sour bread and salt herring?"

Most impelling was the returned villager who had gone to America, succeeded financially, then returned to bring his family to America with him or to claim a bride. In *The Distant Magnet*, an intensely documented record of immigration, Philip Taylor wrote:

> When Klug Anderson Slogvig went back to Norway in 1837, people from all parts of the diocese of Bergen and from Stavanger came to talk with him. . . . Three quarters of a century later, and many hundreds of miles from Scandinavia, the effect was the same. In Italy, the popular attitude was summed up in the words, "They come back arrayed like signori." And an American visitor saw chairs all around the best room of a Sicilian house, to accommodate the people who came, each evening, to hear a returned emigrant's account of his six years in the United States.

Invitations to the Land of Gold

Adrift and without hope in the hardships of a dreary life in the home country, who could resist the tales of prosperity, of tables laden with food, of freedom to speak and to get a job? Who wouldn't yearn for the day when he or she could set out for the fabulous country across the sea?

Anna Vacek, a ten-year-old Czech girl, might stand for millions of young Europeans who yearned for the chance to go for America, a land where anything good might happen to an immigrant. Anna later recalled what her older sister, already in America, had told her:

> I heard somewhere that if you see a star fall down from the heavens, you should make a wish and never say anything to nobody—and you'll surely get your wish.
>
> Well, that was something for me! Every night, I went out to close the door on the geese that I took care of. One evening there was such a beautiful sky with lots of stars. I said, "My dear stars. I wish that I could go to that America."
>
> While I said this, I saw a star falling down to the east. Oh, this is fine! Oh, I wish! I'm going to keep my wish, that's true, and never say anything. I was ten years old. I said nothing to nobody when I saw the star coming down.

Two years later her sister, already settled in America, sent Anna money to come to Ellis Island. The falling star was about to start Anna on her to voyage to America.

Chapter Six

"IT WAS NOT A DESIRABLE PLACE"

When Congress began exploring New York Harbor in 1890 for a site to house a new immigration center, a quick decision was made that an island in the harbor must be the prime target. In such an insular isolation, immigrants could be effectively separated from evil outside influences and could easily be transported to railroad stations by boat.

Bedloe's Island would have been the perfect spot, except that a magnificent symbol of American independence had reached the limited acreage first. In the four years since the Statue of Liberty had been raised on the island, the place had become almost hallowed ground. The statue rose in such towering, eye-catching magnificence that even the thought of sharing Bedloe's Island with any other agency was deemed by most New Yorkers as at least a crime against freedom and at worst, a sin against all humanity.

New York City so cherished Miss Liberty that immediate, bitter anger erupted when Treasury Secretary William Windom suggested early in 1890 that new immigration facilities could be built in her shadow on 12-acre Bedloe's Island. If Windom's suggestion was a mere trial balloon (as many thought it was), it soared higher and more explosively than the naive secretary could have expected.

Joseph Pulitzer and his *New York World* proclaimed that surrounding the statue with buildings "will be to dwarf and humiliate it." Pulitzer's editorial tartly asked: "Cannot something be done in Congress at once to prevent this outrage?" Most New Yorkers envisioned an immigration center as a "babel" that would detract from their newly-won object of affection.

Word of the proposal sped eastward to Paris, where Auguste Bartholdi reacted with horror. He criticized even the notion of any facility next to Miss Liberty as "monstrous" and a "desecration." That Parisian verbal reaction ended all possibility that Bedloe's Island would provide space for an immigration processing center. Attention turned to Governor's Island, a short distance from The Battery.

Governor's Island had been ceded to the United States government and was converted into a U.S. Army base just before the War of 1812. Although by 1890 the island's big guns had outlived their usefulness as a strong deterrent to any enemy, military installations were in place and the island housed Fort Jay. The army let it be known that it would not relinquish the island (and it never has: troops still live at the installation).

That left only Ellis Island, another of the low-lying Oyster Islands like Bedloe's. Native Americans had called the place *Kioshk*, meaning Gull Island, because of the flocks of squawking gulls that frequented the small bird haven. In time, oyster shells mixed with mud to lend some stability to the property.

Governors of New Amsterdam bought the island from the Indians in 1630, thus establishing a claim that New York City would revive 300 and more years later in a quest to establish the city's ownership. Dutch fishermen called the spot Little Oyster Island. Several pirates who were executed by hanging on the island brought another name in 1760. The dead corsairs hung for days from the gibbet (hanging tree). Ergo, the epithet "Gibbet Island" became common.

But by about 1770, on the eve of the American Revolution, Samuel Ellis bought the island to store supplies for his wares—spars for masts, barrels of shad and herrings, cheap twine, and miscellaneous merchandise. Ellis, by the way, continued to call it Oyster Island.

Descendants of Ellis sold the land to the United States government in 1812 as an added armed fortress to thwart the British if they attempted to invade New York City during the War of 1812. The only shot fired in anger there was heard in 1814 when an enlisted man murdered an officer. He was hanged on the island, reinforcing the name Gibbet.

As the years passed, small cadres of federal troops were stationed on the island, which slowly became a storage place for ammunition. Thus the desolate but increasingly dangerous property earned yet another nickname, "powder magazine." Residents in towns along the New Jersey waterfront near Ellis Island worried constantly that a spark might detonate the island and spread devastation across the area.

In January 1890, United States Senator John McPherson of New Jersey introduced a resolution calling on the navy to buy another storage area to house the dreaded explosives. President Benjamin Harrison signed the McPherson bill into law on April 11, 1890. In the same bill, a rider appropriated $75,000 "to enable the Secretary of the Treasury to Improve said Ellis Island for immigration purposes."

Despite his known disdain for the muddy, tide-washed island, Secretary of the Treasury William Windom had the responsibility to use the $75,000 properly to make the place useful. Congress likely did not know of Windom's earlier statement that nothing could be built on the small island, scarcely 100 yards long. Windom, alone among all the participants before the 1890 resolution, had tried to step ashore on Ellis Island, traveling aboard a United States Revenue Service cutter. Foiled by the mud flats nearly at the surface of the harbor, Windom's boat could not get within 150 yards of the island. The secretary later wrote the Joint Committee on Immigration that the island "seemed almost on a level with the water."

The secretary ordered the boat to leave, concluding that "even if we could get rid of the powder magazine which is there now, and could secure the island, it was not a desirable place." He said he had also been so advised by New York City's collector of customs.

But if bureaucratic Washington knew anything of that earlier report, it ignored the warnings and gave Windom the $75,000 to prepare the site for buildings that would follow. The feats that were accomplished by Windom's crew within the stringent budget verged on Herculean:

> A new channel, 200 feet wide, 1,200 feet long, and 12 feet deep to permit immigrant-loaded ferries to approach the island.
> New docks for landing passengers.
> Doubling the island's size by dumping fill behind 860 feet of surrounding crib-walls.
> Digging artesian wells and cisterns to supply fresh water.

With the island doubled in size and supplied with water and a waste disposal system, architects designed the new facility, and building began. Every item used in the building, down to the last nail, had to be brought in by boat from the New Jersey mainland. The logistics, plus the costs of supply and labor, boosted the final cost of the new immigration station to $500,000.

As the building rose slowly through the 20 months it took to complete, the enterprise attracted the constant attention of water-borne "sidewalk superintendents." Steerage passengers enviously eyed the construction from the decks of incoming ocean liners. Others kept track from their hundreds of various-sized boats—freighters, ferries, small coastal sloops, and a myriad other business and pleasure vessels.

The activity could be seen from Battery Park but nothing matched the closer views of the boaters. Barges unloaded huge loads of Georgia pine and spruce wood to frame and finish the all-wood structure. The two-story building was tremendous for the day, 400 feet wide and 150 foot deep. When it was nearly finished, a writer for *Harper's Weekly* described its buff-painted walls, the numerous windows, the picturesque towers on the four corners, and the blue slate roof. He likenec building to "a latter-day watering place hotel."

Outward from the main building, carpenters also hastily erected other, smaller structures for a hospital, a laundry, and a utility plant. Several of the former navy explosive magazine buildings were remodeled into dormitories.

While Ellis Island workers moved rapidly toward full construction, immigrants were processed through the Barge Office near Battery Park, built in 1883 to accommodate cabin class passengers on incoming liners. Steamship companies refused to use the stone building and its corrugated iron annex, preferring the old system of inspecting immigrants at the numerous company piers on both sides of the Hudson River. The building lay virtually unused until the closing of Castle Garden.

Faced with federal orders to unload all steerage passengers at the Barge Office after April 1890, steamship owners had to comply. In the 12 months starting in June 1890, a total of 405,665 newcomers passed through the wretchedly inadequate structure. In a masterpiece of understatement, immigration officials blandly reported that the facilities were "not entirely satisfactory."

As the imposing wooden admittance center rose on Ellis Island, the United States Congress passed a rigidly strengthened, comprehensive immigration law in the spring of 1891. It placed all immigration under federal control as a part of the Treasury Department. A superintendent of the new Bureau of Immigration was charged with rejecting all of those blacklisted in categories established in 1882: prostitutes, Chinese "coolies," and "any lunatic, idiot, or any person unable to take care of himself or herself without becoming a public charge."

The 1891 law added polygamists, anyone with a prison record that stemmed from conviction for "moral turpitude," and anyone suffering from "a loathsome or contagious disease." In a bow to labor unions, the new laws also banned anyone from coming to the United States on a contract and even forbade any employer to advertise in Europe anything construed to encourage immigrants to go to America.

However, the provisions in the law that most affected the arrival of foreigners and eased the load for immigrant officials, was the stipulation that steamship companies had to assume responsibility for inspecting America-bound foreigners before bringing them to the United States. The companies would be responsible for the return of any immigrants rejected in this country.

Ship owners had to prepare manifests on each passenger boarding in Europe—not more than 30 per sheet—that could be cross-checked when the immigrants were examined at the Barge Office (and later at Ellis Island). The required information included name, age, sex, marital status, occupation, nationality, last residence, destination in America, and whether the immigrant could read and write.

Each manifest also asked whether the person leaving his homeland had paid his own passage and had tickets through to his final destination; whether he was under contract to work in the United States; if he had ever been in a poorhouse or prison; if he suffered any deformities or illnesses; and whether he was a polygamist.

Enforcing such rigid controls was nearly impossible at the Barge Office. Immigration officials enthusiastically hailed completion of the Ellis Island facilities during the Christmas season in 1891. As the old year ticked away on New Year's Eve in 1891, excitement mounted. Island officials and staff arrived early on New Year's Day 1892 to receive the first immigrants. Three liners bearing steerage passengers were anchored in the harbor, awaiting the opening of the island. On January 2, 1892, the *New York Times* caught the excitement and the poignancy of opening day:

> There were three steamships in the harbor waiting to land their passengers and there was much anxiety among the newcomers to be the first landed at the new station. The honor was reserved for a little rosy-cheeked Irish girl. She was Annie Moore, 15 years of age, lately a resident of County Cork, and yesterday one of the 148 steerage passengers landed from the steamship *Nevada*.
>
> As soon as the gangplank was run ashore, Annie tripped across it and hurried into the big building that covered almost the entire island. By a prearranged plan she was escorted to a registry desk which was temporarily occupied by Mr. Charles M. Henley, the former private secretary of Secretary Windom. . . .
>
> When the little voyager had been registered, Col. Weber [the Commissioner of Immigration] presented her with a $10 gold piece and made a short address of congratulations and welcome. It was the first United States coin she had ever seen and the largest sum of money she had ever possessed. She said she will never part with it but will keep it as a pleasant memento of the occasion.

It is not known whether Annie Moore kept the gold piece, but if she had, its value would be incalculable. The teenaged Irish lass was accompanied by two younger brothers. When they were all processed, they were whisked away to New York City to join their parents, who had come to America shortly before.

Besides those brought to the island from the *Nevada*, the passengers of the *City of Paris* and the steamship *Victoria* were also landed at the new station. That first day, 700 steerage passengers stepped ashore. The *Times* reporter expressed surprise at "the rapidity with which this number was registered and sent on to their various destinations." He said "it was quite a populous little island about noon, when the steerage passengers from the three big steamships were being disembarked, but within a short time they had all been disposed of."

The first ticket sold by the railroad office on the island was purchased by Ellen King, on her way from Waterford, Ireland, to a small town in Minnesota. Railroad employees complained on the first day that the building was so large it required considerable running on their part to round up passengers. The *Times* reporter said that in view of the numbers of immigrants that the facility must accommodate, "finding fault with its size was like complaining of a circle for being round."

Colonel Weber, first superintendent of the reception center, allowed himself a bit of boasting when he spoke to reporters:

> We can easily handle 7,000 immigrants in one day here. We could not handle half that number at the Barge Office. There the greatest delay was in the baggage department. All that is now done away with, as the baggage department has the whole first floor and the arrangement is perfect.

The island's wharves were built to accommodate immigrant-laden ferries on either side, permitting the landing of newcomers from two boats simultaneously. Immediately after setting foot on the wharf, the immigrants were led to stairs on the south end of the building. They climbed the stairs to a huge room divided into ten aisles, each served by many registry clerks.

After registration, the relatively few foreigners who had to be detained for further testing or study were placed in a wire-screened enclosure. Successful immigrants passed on to a large room where those headed for destinations in the West were directed to one end of the room, with those headed for New York City or New England grouped on the other side. After an interlude permitting immigrants to be found by relatives or friends waiting to take them ashore, they could buy railroad tickets and exchange money. Then, they climbed aboard ferries and were taken to railroad stations for the final lap on their journey to becoming Americans.

The first day seemed to belong to the Irish but Ellis Island personnel knew that nationalities of the incoming tides of people had shifted to the southern and eastern nations of Europe—to Italy and Greece and Russia and the Slavic countries of eastern Europe. Anglo-Saxon immigrants were being replaced by the so-called "new immigrant," with darker complexions and facial features different from the Irish, Germans, and Scandinavians who had long dominated the immigration rolls.

Ironically, the numbers of immigrants began to dip sharply soon after the island opened its doors. In August 1892, a cholera scare caused a sharp dip in the numbers of entering foreigners. Strict quarantines were imposed in all United States ports of entry and steamship companies became wary of transporting immigrants. The stiffened rules of entry slowly pared the ranks of newcomers. The United States economy edged sharply downward in 1892, resulting in the so-called Panic of 1893, followed by several years of economic depression.

Immigration officials in Washington and New York believed that the surging waves of immigration were over. The lowest total in decades, a mere 178,748 immigrants, passed by United States inspectors in 1898. And added to all of the reasons cited above for lowered admittance was a searing disaster on Ellis Island on June 15, 1897.

One of the nine night watchmen on duty smelled smoke at 12:38 a.m. on June 15. Following the smell he saw a small blaze in the northeast battery nearest Battery Park. By the time he sounded the alarm and began rousing other workers on the island, the flames were racing along the walls and leaping upward to the second floor.

All 191 immigrants on the island, 55 of them in the island hospital, were located by a quick-moving staff. The rescuers immediately sought to quell any panic, wrapped invalid patients in blankets, and began moving to a dock where the steamer *John J. Carlisle* was moored. Working together, the island staff and watchmen on the *Carlisle* moved patients and other immigrants to safety on the ship. The last leg of the journey, however, involved moving across the red hot tin roof of the collapsed shed that led to the wharf.

No lives were lost in the roundup of patients. The entire rescue episode required only 17 minutes from the first smell of smoke. But by the time the island was evacuated, the entire structure was enveloped in flames that were easily visible in New York City and along the New Jersey mainland. When dawn broke, the fire was under control, but the ruins of the main building were described as "a tangle of charcoal, battered and rusted iron, and ashes, from which smoke was lazily rising."

No investigation was undertaken. Colonel Stump, commissioner general of immigration in Washington, came by train to New York and was on the island at twilight on June 16. When he returned to the city, he told the press: "We have no theories, and so far as I now know an investigation into the cause will be useless. There is nothing to investigate." It had been felt, even before construction was completed, that the main building was a firetrap.

Stump said he would seek an immediate special appropriation from Congress to rebuild as soon as he returned to Washington. He told reporters that he would insist that the new buildings be brick or stone and as nearly fireproof as possible.

There were several positives during the night of terror. The staff had performed admirably. There had been no loss of life and no panic. Most important, about two-thirds of the installation's records had been found in usable condition.

Against that, there was stark reality. Three steamships carrying about 700 immigrants already were in port and another 7,000 immigrants were known to be on ships bound for New York. There could be no stopping or even stemming the flow.

Temporary plans were in place within a day. The island staff rallied to conduct its examinations at the piers where steamships docked. Those found admissible would be cleared on the spot and sent off to trains or other destinations. Ill persons would be taken to city hospitals and those with communicable diseases would be placed in quarantine on Staten Island. Those detained would be lodged in the Barge Office.

Order of a diminished sort gradually fell into place over a period of many months. Detainees were held on an old steamer, the *Narragansett*, tied up at the Ellis Island ferry slip. The small rooms of the Barge Office once again were used to inspect the incoming immigrants. Area hospitals signed contracts to treat and care for injured or chronically ill patients. The chief negative was the lack of protection from swindlers for those being processed.

A *New York Tribune* report on the Barge Office called it "grimy, gloomy, [and] more suggestive of an enclosure for animals than a receiving station for prospective citizens of the United States."

Few questioned the need for a rapid construction of whatever the government had in mind for Ellis Island. Affecting the decision was the widespread belief among those charged with implementing immigrant acceptance into America: the continuing belief among immigration authorities was that the great waves of European newcomers had peaked and would decline.

A new reception center was authorized a few weeks after the fire. Architects faced the formidable task of providing a fireproof structure with a brick exterior that would combine the functions of a welcoming center, processing area, railroad station, hospital, and for those detained, a suitable holding area. Everything had to be non-flammable—concrete floors, iron beds, and wire netting.

Plans for the new center had an air of spaciousness in the large waiting room and inspection rooms, a restaurant capable of serving thousands of meals daily, hospital wards, a bathhouse, dormitories for more than a thousand men and women, a post office, a customs house, administrative offices, and staff residences.

The main building, brick with white limestone trim, had a three-story central building, flanked on either side by two-story extensions. It was said to be "French Renaissance style" although observers saw variations on other styles. It was 385 feet long and 165 feet wide. Each of the four ornamental towers on the middle three-story section was 100 feet high.

The island's services grew constantly and in subsequent years the installation expanded from the original 3 acres to 27. A hospital for contagious diseases was added, and many other buildings were constructed. Officials said that the facility easily could handle 10,000 people daily. Although that total seemed highly unlikely in the weeks just before the facility was opened, time proved that the estimate was correct, although the adverb "easily" often proved impossible to sustain.

Although not quite finished, the new Registry Hall opened on December 17, 1900, two and a half years after the fire. The first immigrants to land and enter through one of the three huge archways were 654 Italians who had arrived in New York aboard the *Kaiser Wilhelm III.* Soon after, on that first day, steerage passengers from the *Victoria*, *Florida*, and *Umbria* trooped across the gangplanks and started the passage toward entry. A total of 2,251 immigrants, mostly Italians, entered on opening day.

Immigration officials erred seriously in believing that lesser numbers of immigrants would seek admittance in future years. Across the Atlantic, glowing reports of America dominated every country. Ellis Island was not quite ready to welcome them. Dark clouds of incompetence, surliness, and outright thievery darkened the Golden Door.

Early in September 1609, after exploring the river north to what is now Albany, Henry Hudson turned around and headed home. This depicts his ship, the Half Moon, sailing beneath the towering Palisades, which a crew member thought contained precious minerals. (The Christian Century.)

This Dutch map, drawn in 1673, depicted New York after the Dutch recaptured it briefly. Many place names suggest familiar modern areas, such as Lange Eylandt, Greenwyck, Achter Kol, and Manhattan. The Dutch fleet is shown entering the harbor. (Pageant of America.)

*Although importation of slaves from Africa was forbidden after 1808, shiploads of emaciated slaves were smuggled into the United States, packed on decks and in the holds of ships. (*Harper's Weekly.*)*

The last goodbye, as seen by a Harper's Weekly *artist in 1858. Emotions ran high on the docks and on the wooden stairs leading to the deck of the sailing ship. There was only time for one more handshake or one more kiss. Then the ship would ease off into the ocean toward America. (*Harper's Weekly.*)*

Too soon, reality swelled in the minds of those who ventured below decks. This dark, wretched hold would be their fate for from three weeks to two months, depending on the weather and the skill of the crew. This was steerage, the bane of nearly every poor person who crossed on minimum fare. (National Maritime Museum.)

The dazzling view of the New York skyline, not high by modern standards but very impressive in 1870. Ships of all sizes steamed or sailed through the busy harbor. The tallest building was Trinity Church, whose tall steeple shows in the center of the drawing. (Author's collection.)

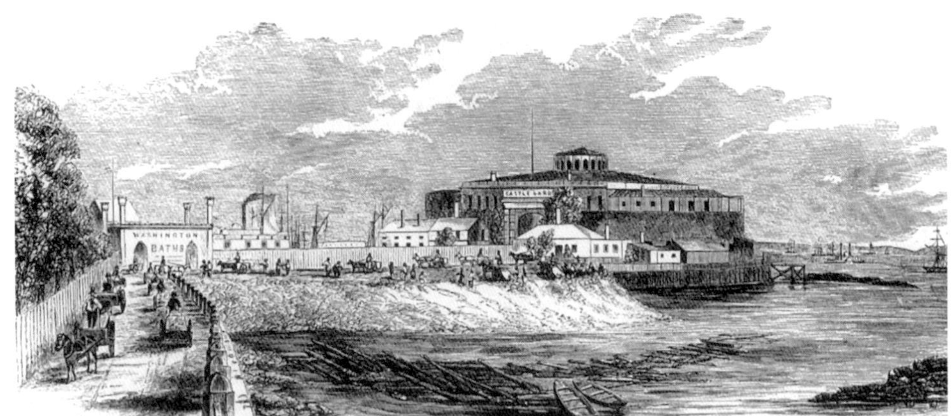

Castle Garden, the round former fort so well known to European immigrants. The city-owned structure had been Music Hall after the fort was abandoned, and the site became the major immigration center for the United States starting in 1855. It served for 45 years. (Author's collection.)

The immigrants streamed ashore, looking totally different from the Americans they would meet and speaking in a wide variety of languages. They were headed for a relatively simple examination and in time they would step into America for real. (Author's collection.)

Frederic Auguste Bartholdi working on Miss Liberty's left hand in his Paris Studio. This was the stage when a plaster of Paris mold was sculpted, to be followed later by the creation of the 200 copper plates that would comprise the statue. (National Park Service.)

The arrival of the Statue of Liberty in crates created the occasion for a huge celebration, as featured here on the front page of Frank Leslie's Illustrated Newspaper *for June 27, 1885. The crated plates were aboard the french vessel* Isere, *the white ship in the left center. (Author's collection.)*

The "new" Ellis Island reception center, opened in December 1900, was said to be capable of handling 10,000 immigrants a day, although no one expected so many would ever arrive at the island. The three-story brick building, trimmed with limestone, was 385 feet long. It was an impressive sight in the harbor. (National Park Service.)

Heavily-laden immigrants left the ferry, trudged across the wooden dock, and entered the front doors of the massive reception center. (Library of Congress.)

Although the song cover doesn't make clear whether the trio approaching the immigrants were friends or thieves, the song "Only an Emigrant" paid tribute to the newcomers in "a beautiful song and chorus." (Library of Congress).

This cartoon was not intended to please aliens, despite Uncle Sam's open-arm welcome to immigrants, who, based on the signs, had arrived only to enjoy no taxes, kings, or compulsory military service—as well as "free education, free land, free speech, free ballot, and free lunch" aboard the "Ark of Refuge." (Library of Congress.)

Another cartoon showed a puritanical admission official, backed by a wide range of representatives of American vice, questioning the morals of a newly arrived "greenhorn" in New York City. (Author's collection.)

Irish peasants posed in front of a crude stone house with the typical thatched roof of the 1880s. Their rock-covered "lawn" was scarcely a place of comfort for those who sat there, but it was at least a refuge from laboring in the potato fields. (Library of Congress.)

Life was simple in Poland when this photograph was taken early in the twentieth century. Father and mother wove baskets in the front yard of their log-cabin type house. (Library of Congress.)

Dressed in their finest native clothing, a young couple was about to leave the Province of Dalarne in Sweden, sometime in the late 1890s. Father donned a formal short coat over his leather apron and mother's long skirt fell across one of the wheels. (Library of Congress.)

In Naples, Italy, departing emigrants were rowed across the harbor to the ship, which was waiting to place them in steerage quarters.

Passengers in the two more expensive classes could look down into the cargo hatch, where steerage passengers were permitted a share of sunlight. (Steamship Historical Society.)

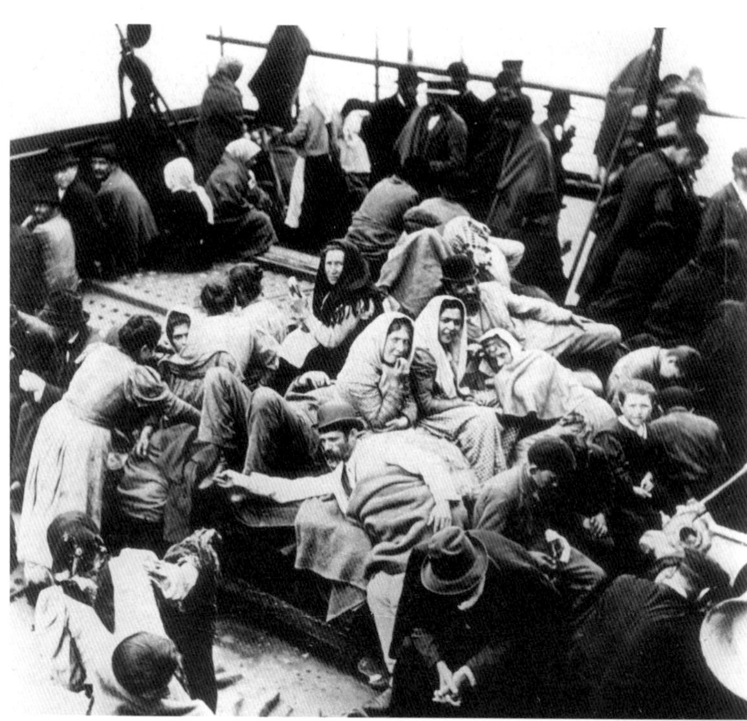

Some steamship lines offered more space for passengers to come up from fetid steerage quarters to enjoy at least a bit of the relaxation afforded first and second class passengers. (National Park Service.)

Finally the long and painful voyage neared an end. Cheers echoed aboard the immigrant ships when passing the Statue of Liberty, mixed with joyous sobbing and thanks that the ship had arrived safely. From the other side of the vessel, Ellis Island would have been visible just ahead. (National Park Service.)

When first and second class cabin passengers had debarked, all the immigrants aboard the ship could gather topside to pose for a portrait. Since each of these passengers paid passage money, however small, the total received by a steamship company was huge. (National Park Service.)

Headed for Ellis Island on the ferry General Putnam, *new arrivals gathered at the railings to catch a glimpse of the island and remained there until the ferry finally docked. It was time to step into a situation that nearly all of them feared—even as they hoped for admittance to the United States. (National Park Service.)*

When immigrants stepped ashore, all their belongings went ashore with them, as in the case of this young Polish newcomer who shouldered his heavy trunk as he entered Ellis Island in 1907. (Library of Congress.)

A mother and son wearing number 18 (their place on the manifest sheet), were bundled against the winter cold while waiting to start the entrance process. (National Park Service.)

This mother tries a shy smile, even as she balances her bundle atop her head. However, her three children cannot hide mingled expressions of fear and wonder. (Library of Congress.)

Maintaining dignity was this immigrant's major goal—and he preserved it with aplomb amidst the noisy, cluttered atmosphere of Ellis Island and the burdens of his luggage, his warm hat, and his long, fur-trimmed coat. (Library of Congress.)

The ordeal was about to begin as each group of manifest passengers began to climb the stairs leading to the Registry Room. As they climbed, doctors looked for signs of weakness or serious disease. They carried their baggage with them. (New York Public Library.)

Eight children, orphaned when their parents were massacred by Russians in October 1907, were shepherded through the immigration process on May 8, 1908. (National Park Service.)

The ordeal that this family was about to endure was frightening as they faced it. The four children wore garments all cut from the same cloth; their mother wore more traditional clothing. All except the baby wore babushkas to cover their hair. (National Park Service.)

The Registry Room, where millions of people faced the questioners who stood between them and admittance to America. The long lines moved between the pipes, facing doctors for the first tests. About 80 percent of all people successfully got through this stage of the admission process. (Library of Congress.)

The most dreaded moment for an immigrant was the eye examination. Eyelids were rolled over so doctors could search for trachoma. Discovery meant deportment, without exception. (National Park Service.)

Patients suspected of having lung diseases were carefully examined after being pulled out during the initial quick study as the immigrants entered the Registry Hall. (Library of Congress.)

A group of well-dressed women kept their faces impassive as young men spoke to them while they were waiting the oral examination that all immigrants dreaded. (Library of Congress.)

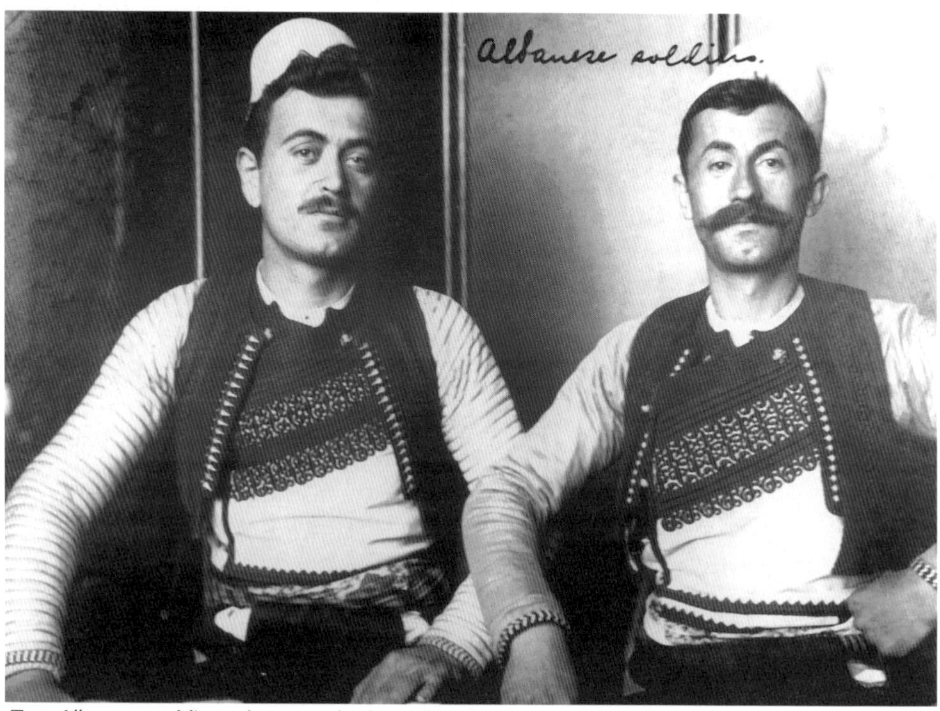

Two Albanese soldiers photographed on Ellis Island wore the kind of colorful clothing and hats that identified their nationalities in the immigration lines but would have been considered inappropriate on the streets of America. (National Park Service.)

Four Dutch children, with well-shined dark shoes, had mixed feelings about the photographer. The boys showed a willingness to smile, but their sisters weren't so sure. (National Park Service.)

A young man whose mental capacity was being tested sought to put various-shaped blocks into their proper holes while a uniformed Ellis Island doctor and an interpreter looked on. (National Park Service.)

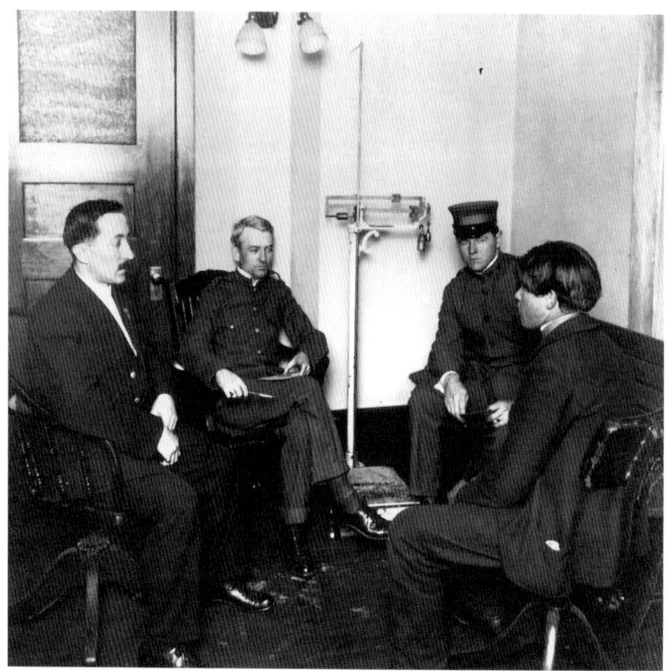

Personal examinations of suspected criminals were common at Ellis Island, conducted by island personnel including trained social service employees and an interpreter. This immigrant could have been detained for anything from anarchism to polygamy. (National Park Service.)

A young man, possibly fearful that he might be subject to further questioning or even deportation, argued with an official as he faced the final questioning. (National Park Service.)

Four glum immigrant children celebrated their first Christmas in America, with the decorations and toys supplied by the Ellis Island staff. (Library of Congress.)

America was very near for these immigrants waiting to change their currency into American money. Instructions and rates were marked on signs at the counter. (National Park Service.)

The final step before leaving the island for railroad terminals in Hoboken and Jersey City was the railroad ticket office, where immigrants could expect fair treatment. America was at hand. (National Park Service.)

This view of the interior of an immigrant car shows the passengers in various stages of preparing food, sleeping, knitting, or looking out the windows. It was more like a huge parlor than a railroad passenger car. (National Park Service.)

An immigrant woman striding along The Battery in her native garb, which would soon be discarded for more "American" garments. (Museum of the City of New York.)

This postcard of New York City's Hester Street in 1898 showed immigrants vying for space at open air markets. This kind of view amazed relatives and friends in Europe: imagine a country where anyone could buy anything at any time! (Museum of the City of New York.)

Groceries and the U.S. mail mixed well in a New York Italian neighborhood. Next door, to the right, a neighborhood bank was available. (Library of Congress.)

Many immigrant children, such as this boy in a Virginia glass factory, never had a chance to be young. In 1911, when this photograph was taken, he worked all night every other week, and all day on the alternate weeks. (Museum of the City of New York.)

An Italian father and mother and their three children assembled artificial flowers in their New York tenement in 1908. They received 6¢ for a gross of finished flowers—24 for a penny. (Library of Congress.)

Immigrant women pause to buy bread from a little boy who carried the loaves from his mother's kitchen. Customers handled the bread, seeking the perfect loaf, with no thought of sanitation. P. Avallone's bicycle shop created the background. (Library of Congress.)

Part of the Americanization process in schools was saluting the flag, as these dutiful children did at the Mott Street Industrial School in New York City c. *1890. (Museum of the City of New York.)*

Photographed in 1926, this group whiled away the hours of waiting at Ellis Island with an impromptu dance. The sign on the wall reads "No charge for meals here," in six different languages. (George Eastman House.)

Chapter Seven

ISLAND OF THIEVES

On the eve of the greatest surge of immigration to America, a festering sickness of corruption and thievery threatened to enmesh Ellis Island in a scandal of monumental proportions. The ensuing investigations reached all the way to the White House, where President Theodore Roosevelt personally and forcefully intervened.

Ironically, the move of immigration procedures to an island was regarded as the cure for the scams and schemes that surrounded immigrants as they left the old center at Castle Garden. Unfortunately, the grip of New York politicians on the entrance process made corruption worse by bringing it inside the center, placing immigrants at the mercy of politically-appointed workers and politically-selected operators of concessions.

Thomas Fichie, politically active New York Republican boss, became the new administrator of the island when it reopened after the 1897 fire. Fichie put one of his henchmen, Edward McSweeney, in charge of day-to-day operations. The floodgates of evil had been opened. Another party activist, labor leader Terence Powderly, became commissioner of the Bureau of Immigration in Washington, D.C.

Powderly distanced himself from the New York politicians. His inspections of the McSweeney operations left him appalled. He denied responsibility, recalling later in his memoirs that the scandal had swollen to disgraceful proportions before he took action. Relatives who wanted to greet immigrants on the island were illegally charged a fee to enter the compound. Immigrants were overcharged at food counters and cheated at the money exchange. Railroad tickets were sold at swollen prices. Employees gleefully relished the little gold mine that politics had created.

Powderly moved forcefully, appointing a committee to investigate. Its report prompted the firing of 11 Ellis Island employees in June 1900. But the national politicians were not quite ready to relinquish their pot of gold.

Edward Steiner, a minister and teacher who made several trips in steerage, masquerading as an immigrant to investigate conditions in steerage and on the island, confirmed and expanded knowledge of the perfidy.

In wide-ranging accusations, Steiner told of "roughness, cursing, intimidation, and a mild form of blackmail" on the island. He described the restaurant, a very profitable enterprise, as "a den of thieves, in which the immigrants were hoodwinked by the operating agency, whose proprietor stole from him as well as the immigrants." Steiner wrote that the bowls and cutlery in the restaurant and the floor were seldom washed. Some immigrants were made to work in the kitchen without pay.

The investigative clergyman told of being robbed of three quarters of the money due him when he traded for a European gold piece at the Money Exchange. Inspectors in the Registry Hall hinted to him that clearance would be much easier if a bribe were offered. Immigrants with large sums of cash were detained, offering the possibility of swindling some of their money from them.

The minister described a "very friendly" inspector who approached him and told him that to insure passage off the island, Steiner should consider that "money judiciously placed might accomplish something." Steiner added another type of an inspector misusing his power:

> A Bohemian girl whose acquaintance I had made on the steamer came to me with tears in her eyes and told me that one of the inspectors had promised to pass her quickly if she would promise to meet him at a certain hotel. In heartbroken tones she asked, "Do I look like that?"

The swindling continued even after immigrants had passed all tests and were admitted. The restaurant concession insisted that the foreigners buy expensive box lunches even if they did not need or want them. Railroad agents sold tickets at highest rates; one immigrant headed for Chicago by a route that took him to New York State and Virginia before heading west.

Newspapers picked up every scrap of information concerning the blatant scandals. In the summer of 1901 headlines told of immigration inspectors who boarded incoming ships at quarantine and sold forged citizenship papers to immigrants, allowing them to bypass Ellis Island. The thieves had gone too far.

President Roosevelt stepped into the picture with the blunt approach that had endeared him to American voters. He wrote a condemnation of Fichie, banding him as "utterly inefficient." Underling McSweeney was labeled "corrupt." Both were summarily removed from their positions of evil power.

On April 28, 1902, Roosevelt appointed William Williams, a wealthy Wall Street lawyer, as commissioner of Ellis Island. Williams greeted island workers with a notice that if they continued their illicit activities they would be fired. He posted a notice throughout the island:

> Immigrants must be treated with kindness and consideration. Any government official violating the terms of this notice will be recommended for dismissal from the service. Any other person so doing will be requested to leave. It is earnestly requested that any violation hereof, or any instance of any kind of improper treatment of immigrants at Ellis Island, or before they leave the barge office, be promptly brought to the attention of the commissioner.

Employees got the message when several non-conforming workers were fired after the notice appeared. Williams's action irked politically powerful forces that ran island concessions. He terminated political contracts in the food, baggage, and money exchange concessions. Roosevelt fully supported Williams. Immigrants could expect fair treatment at the concessions and in the inspection lines.

In a major move, Williams introduced the then-new Civil Service system to Ellis Island to replace the old practice under which jobs were given out in return for personal or political favors, and he established the principle that increases in wages and job status would come from merit rather than favoritism. His goal was to make the system work fairly, according to federal laws, but as time would reveal, not necessarily compassionately toward all foreigners.

Newspapers quickly climbed aboard the Williams bandwagon. On August 7, 1902, *Leslie's Weekly* praised Williams as a "thorough, hard-working and resourceful executive." A few months later, on October 4, 1902, an *Outlook* article said that immigrants were treated with "real tenderness," a considerable exaggeration.

Williams sided with those who wanted to restrict immigration, particularly among people coming from southern and eastern European nations. He candidly believed that their standards did not match those of the Anglo-Saxon immigrants who predominated before 1890. As he pressed to increase the policy of exclusion, many immigrants were excluded who might have qualified under previous administrations. He encountered heavy fire from ethnic groups and from owners of steamship companies.

Roosevelt made a surprise visit to the island on September 16, 1903. His visit cleared Williams, and a commission appointed to study his regime praised him for "the indefatigable zeal and intelligent supervision he has exercised in administering the affairs of the Ellis Island station and the humane considerations he has invariably shown to the immigrants while they remained under his jurisdiction."

Williams resigned in January 1905 to return to his law firm. He was replaced by Robert Watchorn, one-time United Mine Workers official who had entered the United States in 1880 as a steerage passenger. He was admitted at Castle Garden.

Watchorn took office at the high tide of the so-called "Progressive Era," when social-minded men and women pushed for reforms at all levels of government and social welfare. They sought justice for broad segments of the populations, worked to eliminate child labor in factories and mines, and in general became the serious, powerful strong arm of help for the afflicted and helpless. Several of them were given permanent office on Ellis Island.

The island took on a kinder, more honest, and more efficient character under Watchorn. He also concerned himself with the excessive fares and inferior treatment of immigrants after they left the protection of Ellis Island. He sent an island employee, Philip Cowan, disguised as an immigrant to board a westbound immigrant train. Cowan's stinging report of injustice and cheating prompted Watchorn to file a complaint against the railroad with the Interstate Commerce Commission.

Williams returned for a second term in 1909, still determined to run Ellis Island efficiently and honestly but also committed to stricter interpretation of immigrant laws. He insisted that "it is necessary that the standard of inspection at Ellis Island be raised," and also urged immigration officials abroad to inform prospective emigrants of the high standard of immigration laws that would be enforced as they landed in America. Williams paid particular attention to "paupers" and anyone "likely to become a public charge."

Neither Williams nor Watchorn could totally eliminate injustice and cheating, but their principles brought an honest effort to stabilize Ellis Island, although many employees remained surly and hostile to immigrants. Part of the reason was the never-ceasing flow of humans from Europe, desperately hoping to become Americans—and often desperately trying the patience of even conscientious employees who sought to make the entrance pleasant.

Chapter Eight

GOODBYE TO THE HOMELAND

Viewing life in much of late nineteenth-century Europe solely from the physical and economic aspects, the wonder is not that so many left their villages and cities but rather that so many desperate people preferred to stay in their native hovels, defying pitiful and precarious incomes, diseases, tyranny, and army service for young men. The answer might well be best expressed in the song "Tradition," the opening theme in the musical *Fiddler on the Roof*.

The musical, however beautifully staged or screened, is the cruel story of Russian Jews who lived not only in everlasting poverty but also in dread that at any moment Cossacks might drive them from their homes. The opening song "Tradition" explains why they stayed in their villages, enmeshed in the folklore of hundreds of years of living and dying, of hoping and despairing. It was as much inertia as tradition; poverty and suffering were accepted as the norm. Ties to the home were compelling, usually breakable only by unbearable danger or other desperation.

Thus they lived on, tilling the same impoverished soils that their great-great grandparents had struggled to make productive. They endured wretched army life, faced unrelenting persecution from the rich and powerful, rose at dawn's first light and retired in twilight's glow. Their work left them with little to show beyond a lifetime of drudgery.

With "Come to America" invitations posted from the Ural Mountains to Rotterdam, from Oslo to Naples, and all places between, nearly all Europeans knew of America's amazing wealth and opportunity. They knew as well of Castle Garden or Ellis Island, the gateways to whatever dreams of America they cherished, be it freedom, opportunity, gold, or a bit of land of their own. But knowing and leaving were far from synonymous. Often the leaving would be years in the making, and sometimes in a village such as that in *Fiddler on the Roof*, departure could become, overnight, a panicky flight from imminent peril.

Except for the huge numbers of Jews driven from their homes and villages by Russian cruelty and slaughter, most of the departures were planned with the knowledge available. Often, when young family members decided to go to America, older family members would try to keep them at home. The arguments for remaining round fears of what might happen in America: a strong belief persisted among peasants that Native Americans still roamed city streets in the New World. Family attachments and traditions were deep rooted. Elders nursed false hopes that prosperity soon would come to their homeland, and the natural fear of journeying toward the unknown delayed most of the emigrants. One immigrant said that his father was certain "they will put snakes in your bed."

Departures often were hastened by funds coming from immigrants who had previously settled in America, prospering sufficiently to send home money or tickets. Between 1893 and 1903, an estimated $95 million flowed from America to Austria-Hungary. Amounts sent to Italy at about the same time were equally large; nearly $100 million sent back by one-time Italian neighbors now able to save bits of money in America.

In the 1890s, the Hamburg and Bremen shipping lines declared that many immigrants traveling to America on their lines had been subsidized by pre-paid tickets purchased in America. The money helped would-be emigrants and served as well to stimulate great interest in a European village whenever American dollars arrived.

In *The Maiden Voyage*, Geoffrey Marcus provided a realistic look at the young Irish men and women fleeing from the homeland. He chose the port of Queenstown, a favored embarkation point for those turning their backs on centuries of tradition and superstition:

> Queenstown, it has been said, "is a wound which Ireland cannot stanch; and from it flows a constant stream of her best and her youngest blood." For well over a hundred years this stream has been pouring overseas to swell the population of North America, more especially of the United States.
>
> It was a cruel, but imperative uprooting, for the truth was there was nothing for them at home. With mingled grief and hope they would set out on the great adventure of their lives, bound for the land of opportunity—in all probability never to see Ireland again. With a handful of dollars in their pockets, they would plunge into the fiercely competitive life in the New World.
>
> A few, a very few, of them would make their fortunes over there; and, in course of time, merge with the American middle and upper classes. The great majority would toil for meager wages until the end of their days, thankful if only they had a roof over their heads and food for themselves and their children.

If young couples in any European country were married or contemplating marriage, the man often would go alone to test the ordeal of departure and the factors involved in settling down in America. He would promise to return for his wife as soon as possible or to send money for her and other members of his family to join him across the ocean. Except for the trauma of casting aside the past, couples or families normally proceeded with whatever speed suited their philosophies and their courage.

Single women had problems that males could not know or understand. In Europe, many females were overworked beyond endurance for tiny wages. Nothing that America could offer could possibly be worse. In her book *Immigrant Women*, Maxine Schwartz Seller tells of a 16-year-old Swedish miss in the late nineteenth century:

> I had to work like a wolf, go out and spread manure and fertilizer, and on the worst snowy days in winter carry water to eleven cows. This was beside all the house work. I worked every minute from 6:00 a.m. to 9:00 p.m. The hired man has his own room to go to when he has finished work, and then he has noonday rest, but what rest has a maid?

For all her work and all her woes, that Swedish teenager received $7.50 a year! She found it hard to believe that in America someone might make that much in a week, or more realistically for females, two weeks.

Economic enslavement was not the only reason for women fleeing European villages. Married women occasionally migrated to escape abusive husbands. Many young women left their home countries to avoid an unwanted marriage. Irish girls especially recognized that poverty followed most marriages in their homeland.

After selling their meager holdings, married couples, as well as single persons, stepped into the unknown, regardless of what letters from America said or what shipping and railroad agents declared in their glossy invitations to potential emigrants. First, those fleeing Europe had to get to the nearest port of embarkation, which as often as not was hundreds of miles away. Usually they set out on foot or in crude wagons. If they had enough money, they would head for the nearest railroad station to board a train.

The journey to the embarkation point might take many days or many weeks, along paths fraught with danger. In winter, the paths and roads could be covered with deep snow. In spring, mud would make walking difficult and in summer, intolerable heat would slow the infirm and the elderly.

Hoodlums lurked along every popular road, eager to snatch valuables from defenseless emigrants. If there were few valuables, the assailants could inflict crippling injuries or even death on unfortunate victims. Brutal thieves usually went for a traveller's neck, knowing that the emigrants carried their cash in bags suspended around the neck.

Departing families cut their ties to their neighbors, their villages, and their heritage. The tiny windfalls they gained by selling their homes and furnishings (for sums averaging about $300) had to be hoarded, to pay for the voyage to America, and ultimately as proof to Ellis Island officials that they would not become public charges.

Those leaving could take to America only what they could wear or carry. Women often became walking wardrobe closets by donning several petticoats and dresses, topped by multiple sweaters or coats, giving them the appearance of being exceptionally obese.

Each person could carry a suitcase or bundle—so planned that its contents would take the holder to the port of departure and beyond to their first days and weeks in America. The bundle would be their sustenance, their revered remembrance of their homelands, and a small grip on the unknown future. Choosing what to take and what to leave had to be an agonizing summing up of a life.

Each immigrant, down to the smallest child who could walk, carried items as varied as each individual taste. Many packed bulky feather mattresses, which could take up more than half the space in a trunk. There were those who would pack a large salami, bologna, or sausage, doubtful that America could offer anything so precious. Some brought trinkets, blankets, or books. Many packed bottles of expensive homeland whiskey, then learned to their consternation that much better brands of whiskey could be bought in America for far less money.

A bundle might contain articles of clothing or nightwear. More often than not, the clothing that was so stylish in a European village would be considered garish, cheap, or ill-fitting by American fashion. There was no standard to be followed. No magazine articles or travel books offered the kinds of advice modern tourists get for even a long weekend in the Bahamas. A Bible was quite standard in the suitcases or bundles of emigrants.

Many tales of leaving can be found in Ellis Island files or in interviews conducted when most immigrants had attained middle age or beyond. One example, recorded in the fine book of interviews by David and Douglas Brownstone and Irene Franck, *Island of Hope, Island of Tears*, encapsuled the process of leaving in an interview with Celia Rypinski, who was in her mid-80s when asked to recall the early stages of her immigration that took place in about 1908. Her brother John had established himself in America and sent her money to join him. Celia recalled the departure from her native Poland when she was 13 years old:

> I went with my brother to the border of Poland, to Germany. . . . Up to that time I had never seen a train. I saw such a big train, tracks and train, and I said, "What is that?" And my brother said, "You're going to ride on one like that, maybe a couple of hours. You'll find out what they are."
>
> I had with me a basket of linens that my brother (in the United States) had paid for—I was to come and bring it, bedding and everything. But my bother, he turned his horses and the wagon and went back home—and took my trunk! The basket I had everything in! My brother in Poland wrote after a while that he could not mail it because I had the ticket [for the basket] with me.

Celia's train halted in Berlin for two days to observe a German holiday. She remained on the train until it resumed the journey to Rotterdam, where Celia boarded the ship that took her to America. She could neither read nor write, but she eventually made her way from Ellis Island to Chicago, being aided along the way by a sign she wore on her chest. That badge of travel, in several different languages, gave her name, her nationality, and her destination.

Ports of embarkation were well placed along the north European coasts and off the Mediterranean Sea. They were not numerous and had to be large enough to house and process immigrants waiting for their ships and to berth and service the huge steamships that by 1890 carried most steerage immigrants to Ellis Island.

Some of the ports, such as Liverpool, had been transporting English, Irish, and Scotch immigrants for decades. Others, such as Bremerhaven or Hamburg in Germany, Rotterdam in Holland, and LeHavre in France, also had many years of experience in handling the departing individuals and families. Southern Europeans headed for ships in less-experienced Piraeus, Riga, Milan, Naples, Trieste, and Fiume.

A family might pool meager funds to permit a crippled or handicapped member of the family to travel second class on the steamship, whereby he or she would be admitted to America without question. In steerage, rejection would be certain.

If laws were followed carefully in the sending ports, each potential immigrant was examined closely by government bureaucrats and steamship company doctors. Theoretically, owners of the vessels were supposed to eliminate in Europe anyone certain to be rejected at Ellis Island. In practice, the profits made on each individual were enough to permit some emigrants to slip through the European net who were certain to be rejected in America. It was a cruel treatment for the affected individuals, but business was business and profits were irresistible.

It is well to remember that would-be immigrants rejected at Ellis Island were returned only to their port of debarkation. It could be hundreds or more miles from the village in which the immigrant had resided. Being returned to Bremerhaven, for example, for a Russian Jew who had escaped a pogrom in his home village far to the east was about the same as being dropped in the middle of Sodom or Gomorrah.

And so they hastened up the steep gangplanks to gaping doors in the side of the ship. They entered, then carried their scant possessions down into the bowels. There was little effort to provide guidance as the frightened, bewildered people sought to find their places—or even a place where they might lay down their heavy baskets or suitcases.

This, after all, was not a cruise on the Mediterranean or to the Scandinavian fjords. This was a voyage into unknown terrors and, hopefully, into the dreams of fulfilled privileges and prosperity.

The whistles on the stacks blew, the steam engines throbbed, steerage teemed with life. The vessel was tugged away from the dock, then set free from the tugs to answer the call of the engines. Ahead, far across the surging ocean, lay that place called America. Somewhere on that distant shore lay Ellis Island. Somewhere in that distant continent there had to be opportunity.

Chapter Nine

DOWN TO THE VERY BOTTOM

Reality assaulted the senses as soon as an immigrant stepped into the darkness and the stench of steerage, where they would be crowded together until America was reached. Smells of the vomit of those who had traveled before mingled with the smells of the cattle, wood, and grains that comprised the cargo on most ships when they returned to Europe.

Immigrants were considered just another cargo, even if human beings were more complicated to handle than cattle or wood. Thus immigrants were overseen by the United States Treasury Department until 1903, when they were consigned to the new Department of Commerce and Labor.

Steerage was in the very bottom of a ship, not far from the furnaces that produced the steam power to drive the big ships and the steering mechanism that guided the ship on a voyage. It was where cattle might have been herded aboard on an eastbound voyage. The space was scarcely fit for even a steer, and only lightly cleaned when the animals were guided ashore. Immigrants would replace them on a ten-day to three-week voyage westward across the Atlantic Ocean. Even as they boarded the ship and headed downstairs toward their accommodations, the gentle rocking of the vessel prompted forebodings of seasickness.

First and second class passengers, generally known as "cabin class," went topside. First class passengers were taken aboard after all others were loaded, lest they be offended by the mass of poor humanity. Luxuries abounded for those in first class. Food was plentiful, tasty, and planned to coax latent appetites into normalcy. Second class accommodations were less luxurious but the food and the berthing were generally good.

Tales of the crossings numbered in the millions; surely every passenger remembered the details of his or her own crossing. Down in steerage they found want, suffered a claustrophobia they could never have imagined at home, and learned of evils unknown to them before the crossing. In steerage they slept in desperately crowded quarters, ate little (and at times) strange food, bore children, conceived other children who would be born in America, picked up rampant communicable diseases, and saw children and others die before their eyes. The dead would be consigned to the sea in perfunctory burials.

There are many tales of kindnesses from other immigrants and even, on rare occasions, from crew members. There are far more tales of cruelty or sexual assault on the part of ship employees who were trusted to protect the passengers. There was unquestioned venality or callous forgetting of promises on the part of many steamship owners, whose fortunes mounted whether they delivered the cargo dead or alive.

Island of Hope, Island of Tears gives a concise account of accommodations in this very worst part of a ship:

> A typical steerage compartment consisted of a compartment, indistinguishable from any upper cargo hold, without portholes or any effective ventilating device, unpartitioned and six to eight feet high, crammed with two or more tiers of narrow metal bunks containing minimal mattresses. Men and women were separated, sometimes on separate decks, sometimes by nothing but a few blankets tossed over a line in the middle of the compartment.
>
> Toilet facilities were always inadequate; cleanup was almost non-existent; and the combined smells of the galley and human excrement nauseating. The food was both monotonous and poorly prepared—if prepared at all—and fresh water was usually available only up on deck. The chief kind of food provided described by many immigrants, was barrel after barrel of herring, the cheapest food available that might be relied on to keep the immigrants alive.
>
> Under those conditions, people got seasick and stayed seasick. They cried and kept on crying. Some people were even detained at Ellis Island later for suspected trachoma, when their eyes were simply red from continued crying all the way across the Atlantic.

Immigrant ships were little changed for nearly a century. By the 1840s and 1850s, when great masses of Irish and German immigrants arrived in America, ships were larger but still depended on billowing sails for power. Navigation instruments were much improved but savage storms and even long periods of dense clouds cut deeply into their efficiency. In the earliest days, livestock and other items were placed on the upper deck, limiting the ability of passengers to walk freely. Below decks there was only moderate change from colonial days. There was much greater room available, which essentially meant that more people could be crowded into the newly created space. The misery per passenger was about the same.

Food was always a major problem, regardless of the era in which an immigrant set forth for America. In the 1850s, when passengers supplied their own food, there are records of immigrants buying and taking aboard ship stores to last for a month or more. The larder generally would contain edibles likely to last for a long time, such as beans and rice. Occasionally an individual might add such luxuries as lemons, figs, or spices.

Prudent people bought barrels or boxes for the foodstuffs and canisters for the tea and coffee, as well as chamber pots, cooking utensils, a lantern, pots and pans, cheap dishes, and inexpensive cutlery. Passengers were expected to cook such food as they could, often difficult because of the crowds of would-be cooks and hungry people gathered around the stoves.

There obviously was no planned entertainment. Passengers could sit and listen to the groaning of the ship's timber, hear the howling winds of a North Atlantic winter storm, or the shouts of sailors adjusting the sails. Still there were some irrepressible young people who would push back moveable barrels and beds and dance or jig to the tune of a violin or concertina. Children and adults alike found some pleasure in cards or dominoes.

Sickness was rampant on board ships of the pre-1850 period. However, despite the tightly packed vessels, the death rate (not counting shipwrecks and fires) was relatively low, averaging perhaps 300 or less per year except for one monumental year. That was 1847, when nearly 17,000 deaths at sea were recorded in a study by Quebec officials. By the 1860s, the death rate was about 1 percent among all passengers. Corpses were wrapped in sailcloth weighted with a bag of sand, placed on a board and then, after a brief service read by the captain or a literate passenger, were tipped into the sea. Children might be placed in a rough, hand-made, sand-weighted casket for dumping into the ocean.

Fannie Kligerman, one of those quoted at length in *Island of Hope, Island of Tears*, had suffered from Russian pogroms and the long flight to a port of embarkation. She was 13 years old when she fled to America and one of her lasting memories was the water that flooded the floors of steerage. If that were not enough, nearly all of the children in the group were stricken with measles. Fannie described the omnipresent specter of death:

> Some of them died and they threw them into the water like cattle. It was a pathetic thing that they couldn't ride with the bodies; they had to throw them into the water. It is something that I will never forget. And you can imagine how the women carried on. They took a child from them and they just tossed it in, nice and quiet. It was terrible.

> And my mother hid [her] baby, I remember, in a big apron. She wouldn't let anyone see the baby. Maybe the baby was going to catch it. So she hid the baby in her apron and the baby could hardly walk and was crying. We had to say, "Sh, sh. Somebody's coming, sh." All the time, and that's how we struggled.

Steamships gradually edged aside the sailing vessels. By 1870, larger steam-powered ships were dominating the immigration trade. Such a ship might carry 250 to 300 cabin class passengers and 1,000 to 1,500 immigrant passengers. These larger vessels could average nearly 20 knots but were nearly as likely to wallow in heavy seas as their predecessors.

Steamships grew ever larger as the twentieth century approached. A few extended over 500 feet in length, then 600 feet, until finally, in 1807, the acclaimed, awesome *Mauritania* was launched by the Cunard Line of England. She was 762 feet long, and carried 563 second- and 1,138 third-class passengers. There seldom was anyone listed as steerage—although third class represented a lower class accommodation that immigrants still called steerage.

Many of the steamships carried more than 2,000 persons in steerage. No company was more blatantly immigrant-attuned than the Hamburg-America Line. Two of its ships, each with a distinctively American name, the *President Lincoln* and the *President Grant*, each carried 3,000 immigrants. There were relatively few first- or second-class passengers. Immigrants obviously were a far better cash producer for the German company.

Even the White Star Line, builders of the mighty *Titanic*, planned "permanent third class open space" for immigrants. But in the final plan, most of that space contained rooms advertised as "portable 3rd., White Star pattern," a company system of partitions enclosing open space in steerage. Some portion of the third-class area was the traditional "open space" so abhorred by immigrants.

Third-class ticket holders on the *Titanic's* first (and too soon, only) voyage carried boarding passes that identified them as "immigrant and steerage passengers." British subjects were quickly directed to their quarters but "aliens"—predominantly Scandinavians—were inspected at length. Several persons in third class were journeying to America to join relatives already there.

Goeffrey Marcus, in *The Maiden Voyage*, described the immigrant (third-class) quarters aboard the *Titanic*. His description was in vivid contrast with tales of quarters aboard traditional immigrant vessels. The immigrant area on the acclaimed White Star liner was far and away the Rolls Royce of the steerage world. Marcus also set the rationale for the improved immigrant quarters as being in a shipping company's best interest:

> The quarters provided for the third class on board the Titanic had improved beyond all recognition. They were well ventilated, well heated, and brightly lit by electricity. The third class dining room was situated where the vessel's motion was least felt. The third class also had their own smoking-room, and enclosed promenade, divided with chairs and tables, which could be used in any weather. Berths were clean and comfortable. The food was good, if plain; and there was plenty of it.
>
> All this cost only a few pounds for the trip. It was a wonderful value for the money. It was good business for the company, too. Great liners could not live by millionaires alone. Without the continually increasing and lucrative emigrant traffic, in fact, it would have been economically impossible to operate these mammoth luxury liners.

Immigrants of many nationalities vied for tickets on the maiden voyage. There were Norwegians, Swedes, Danes, English, Irish, Russians, Finns, Poles, Dutchmen, Spaniards, Italians, Greeks, Rumanians, and others in steerage, almost a cross-section of all those landing at Ellis Island from all ships.

There were first-trip problems, of course. Immigrants crowding aboard the mighty ship complained that they were given little information to help them find their accommodations. The more adventurous who sought to climb stairs leading toward first- and second-class cabins found a wire screen barring the way. It seemed a minor, and probably expected, inconvenience as the *Titanic* sailed triumphantly from Southampton, England on April 12, 1912.

Two nights later, as most English-speaking people know (or at least the millions who have seen the movie), the mighty "unsinkable" vessel struck an iceberg in the North Atlantic and sank with a loss of 1,500 passengers and crew members. Nearly all of the third-class passengers died, frustrated in many cases by the screens across the stairwells.

By the time Ellis Island was opened in 1892, the immigrant trade was a proven money maker for all steamship lines. By 1910, steamships carried huge numbers of immigrants in their lower regions, openly calling the facilities steerage or sometimes thinly disguised as "third class." By any name, the quarters were much inferior to those on the upper decks, where passengers slept, ate, and frolicked in style or enjoyed the warm sun as they reclined away the hours in deck chairs.

Many of the ships carrying southern Europeans to America were still relatively small in size. Italian immigrants were packed densely into the holds, never knowing that there were better ships on other, albeit far distant, lines.

The basic change for any immigrant journeying on one of the newer steamships was that he or she arrived in America faster. Many of the bigger ships could cross the Atlantic in 12 days or less between ports. The smaller ships steaming out of the Mediterranean and laboring into the Atlantic seldom made the trip in less than 21 days. The difference, from an immigrant's viewpoint, was that the misery was of shorter duration.

Steerage was a location, rather than an evidence of the quality of the accommodations. Philip Taylor, in *The Distant Magnet*, addressed this facet of the crossings:

> The question that must be asked is, how far the favorable effects of this speed on emigrants' welfare was balanced by the great numbers carried, or by unfavorable factors in ships' design. . . .
>
> Emigrants had of course been inspected, with varying degrees of thoroughness, before embarkation. All ships carried hospitals and doctors, qualified men, even though it was admitted that the best were unlikely to go to sea, and it was hard to guarantee the zeal with which they would perform their duties. In studying immigrant conditions, therefore, it is discomfort that has to be looked for, rather than deadly danger, but it is not easy to determine how severe that discomfort was.

The answer to the question of comfort ranged from the agonies of crossing the Atlantic in a sailing ship to the miseries encountered on the newer, larger, and faster steamships. Edward A. Steiner, author of the classic *On the Trail of the Immigrant*, published in 1906, and an outspoken critic of the handling of immigrants, travelled often in steerage crossings and turned a phrase that likely drew hosannas from those who endured steerage in the supposedly improved days of steam travel: "The steerage of the modern ship ought to be condemned as unfit for the transportation of human beings."

Immigrants had ample reason to believe, from the glowing promises of the steamship brochures, that food would be at least adequate on the larger ships. It was not to be. Most innocent steerage passengers believed that when they bought a ticket they were also buying a berth for the passage. They were, in actuality, merely buying a section somewhere in steerage. A berth in such a section might be shared by as many as four people.

As might be expected, particularly in that age of great modesty, women suffered especially from the lack of privacy. On many ships there were few toilets and seldom more than one for every 100 passengers. Many women on seeing the lack of privacy wept in despair, proclaiming that they never would have undertaken the trip if they had known of the lack of toilet facilities.

Perhaps even worse was the practice on board most ships of berthing men and women together. It was common for women to sit up all night on the floor or on boxes rather than endure the necessity of sharing a berth with a strange man.

Unmarried women suffered in other ways. For one thing, it was difficult for them to get food if there was no male to speak for her. A doctor who often had cared for immigrants in steerage on ships sailing between Liverpool and America told of going into the section on stormy days, bringing water and hard biscuits to women to save them from starvation or dehydration.

More than a half million unmarried, non–English-speaking young women emigrated to America between July 1, 1910 and June 30, 1915. Most of them were under 21 years of age. A woman traveling alone in the nineteenth century was morally suspect and was assumed likely to become a public charge unless she could prove that there was someone in America who would care for her.

A young woman traveling alone could expect at least mild flirtation from crew members and from male immigrants. Matters frequently went beyond mere ogling or leering. The Massachusetts Commission on Immigration, investigating steamship transportation in 1913, found that on one ship, "Polish girls were forced to defend themselves against the advances of the crew, who freely entered the women's dormitory and tried to drag the girls into the crew's quarters."

Other terrors beset both men and women in steerage. Disease was rampant. Cholera, typhus, smallpox, measles, diphtheria, and other highly contagious diseases swept through the crowded, vermin-infested lower regions of a ship. Hundreds of people could become infected: some would die, unattended by any professional help.

John Chamberlain, president of the London Board of Trade, offered a peculiar excuse for some poor conditions found on ships and reported his conclusions in an 1881 document. He maintained that the standard of steamship quarters should not be a comparison to the habits and tastes of middle-class Englishmen [in cabin class] but rather had to be measured against the standards of "the crowded cottage of the English laborer, the close, narrow garret of a workman, or the cabin of a Connemara peasant." In short, travelers with little money were as well served as they expected or deserved.

The report that carried Chamberlain's comments revealed that many steamships had no washrooms in steerage and that passengers had to supply their own bedding and tableware. When considering washrooms and the lack of privacy in nearly every aspect of the steerage accommodations, the investigators undoubtedly relied on their upper middle-class standards. They concluded there was little cause for concern, since in their patronizing belief, emigrants were unlikely to wash anyway and were not accustomed to undressing before going to bed. Lack of privacy for such people, the investigators concluded, was therefore not a hardship.

Based on the nearly unanimous viewpoint of immigrant passengers, food was both meager and tasteless for steerage passengers. The kitchen and eating areas were considered by most ship owners prime places for adding to a ship's income. Since shipping companies were paid in full for all meals, each meal that was not eaten represented greater profit. Thus a heavy storm, certain to induce vomiting, nausea, and a lack of appetite, was, from an owner's economic standpoint, something to be desired.

Fanny Kligerman had this remembrance of the diet aboard the ship in which she crossed: "On the boat they gave us food. They charged plenty, but we didn't go in for it. I still have the herring taste in my mouth. Herring, herring, herring! And garlic, on bread. They say you don't vomit when you have garlic on bread."

Herring was really a matter of opinion, but it is a theme that ran through almost every immigrant's memory. Being very young seemed to make the fish more palatable. Wanda Mary Dombrowski (also cited in *Island of Hope, Island of Tears*), remembered one thing about her voyage: "We didn't come first class, we came third class [which was really about the same as steerage]. There was plenty of herring that you could eat. The food was delicious. I remember so well that great big barrel of herring. I didn't get sick. We could eat the herring any time we wanted to."

Wanda did not become seasick, but it is not difficult to imagine the reaction if a bubbly, lively little seven-year-old brought some of that magical herring into the area of steerage where seasickness was the assailing milieu of the voyage.

Nausea and vomiting, major contributors to the horrid odors in steerage, were universal, not primarily because of steamship company economic policies and negligence but because a rocking boat has since time began been almost certain to bring on seasickness for most passengers. The condition cast a pall over every ship, even in first and second class.

Ann Novotny, in *Strangers at the Door*, shaped a vivid description of life in steerage around an anonymous young (and, based on his vocabulary, apparently well-educated) Russian immigrant who crossed to Ellis Island in 1895:

> The immigrant quarters was a large egg crate, with three tiers of cubicles for bunks and with just enough room in the center to move about before climbing in and out of our beds. Even on clean ships, the overcrowding, stale air, odors of disinfectants, and lack of hot soapy water made all clothes and possessions stink for months after landing.
>
> [There was] an olfactory phenomenon known to all transatlantic travelers of those days as the smell of a "ship." This pervasive, insidious odor, a distillation of bilge and a number of less identifiable putresensces, settled on one's person, clothes, and luggage and stayed there forever, impervious to changes of habitat, clothing, and the cleansing agents available to the poor. It was many years before I realized that only steerage passengers smelled of "ship."

Optimism began to spread through steerage when a crew member told the immigrants that landing was close. A more reliable sign was the sight of the first gull trailing behind the ship, hoping for some first-class galley food or even steerage herring. The lone gull would soon become a flock, flapping behind the ship and squawking a raucous welcome. Land had to be near.

Arrival in New York harbor and the preparations to land ended the agony of steerage and lifted every spirit. Brownstone and Franck, in one of their extensive interviews in *Island of Hope, Island of Tears*, quoted Irene Meladaki Zambelli, who had left Greece in February 1914 at age 24. She remembered forever her ship's arrival in the harbor 22 days later:

> We finally arrived in New York and the Hudson River on March the third. There was no more seasickness and we got ready to leave the ship. We were all dressed up, Sarah not as much as I was. I had a very pretty suit and an embroidered blouse under it and a little hat to match the suit with a pretty bow on it custom made.

On a clear day when the gulls flew, immigrants would come up on whatever deck space was allocated to them. They would pass the diminishing hours in the fresh air with discussions about what questions might be asked on Ellis Island, how much money was needed, whether physical examinations were thorough. Worst of all, they wondered, what would happen if a family member were rejected by the Ellis Island staff?

South of The Narrows in New York Harbor, with no land yet in sight, a pilot from the Sandy Hook Pilots Association would come aboard to guide the ship to a designated dock in New York City or to docks at Hoboken or Jersey City in New Jersey.

Every passenger vessel stopped at quarantine to permit a doctor to board. This would be the point where first- and second-class passengers received a superficial medical examination, the test of their fitness to become American residents. Obviously-ill passengers, in all classes, might be pulled aside and taken ashore for intense physical examination at the quarantine facility on Staten Island.

After passing through quarantine, the full sight of New York City's huge presence unfolded. Then, almost magically it seemed, there she was: the towering, magnificent Lady with the Lamp, the Statue of Liberty. Seeing her loom out of the darkness as dawn broke across the water was a sight never to be forgotten.

The ship sailed northward toward the tall towers of New York City. Its buildings in 1900 were not really high by today's standards, but far higher than anything ever seen by a European peasant. The skyline was about to change notably: the new Singer Building, finished in 1907, would rise 47 stories high, a remarkable sight even by current assessments.

The ship might move slightly eastward off the southern tip of Manhattan to seek a pier in the East River somewhere near the great Brooklyn Bridge finished in 1883. Many other ships docked along the many piers on both the New Jersey and the New York sides of the Hudson River.

First- and second-class passengers were unloaded at the piers. Then the steerage people would either be unloaded or, on particularly busy days, their vessel would proceed down harbor and await her turn to unload the immigrants.

Chapter Ten

THE WORLD'S MOST AWESOME ISLAND

The last leg of the journey to Ellis Island from the pier where first- and second-class passengers debarked could range from only an hour or two to a full day or more, depending on the landing pressure at the island. If the Hudson River was crowded with immigrant steamships, as it often was after 1900, it could take additional days of agonized waiting before Department of Naturalization ferryboats or barges took the fearful immigrants to Ellis. Every additional hour added to the torment of doubt and fear burning within them.

Would the dreaded unknown island open the doors to America or would it merely smash immigrant hopes and force them back to Europe? Would these foreigners answer the questions about money and employment wrongly, creating questions about their ability to survive fiscally in America? Would shipboard rumor that predicted an ordeal on Ellis Island become truth?

Island of Hope, Island of Tears eloquently summed up the swirl of emotions as the boats neared the Ellis Island dock:

> Journey's end—and a new beginning. Behind them a world of police, borders, visas, permits, and all the multiple oppressions only the poor and the oppressed know. Ahead, a wide new continent and the taste and touch of freedom.
>
> Of course the streets were not paved with gold. Certainly the new world exhibited many of the worst features of the old and added crass materialism and new bigotries of its own. But for the vast majority of the tens of millions who came, Ellis Island was literally and symbolically the end of a long, often extraordinarily difficult journey to freedom.
>
> It was a nexus, a whirlpool of forces, people, contending ideas. It was a place where the long-growing, deeply felt idea of a free and open America came into sharp and irreconcilable conflict with an equally old and strong tradition of bigotry in America; where industry's idea of an unending

> supply of cheap labor clashed head-on with organized labor's attempts to protect the jobs of its members.
>
> And it was a place where earlier immigrants tried to help the new arrivals—often their own relatives and neighbors from the old countries—and where millions of people from all over the world came to the America of their hopes and dreams, knowing little or nothing of the maelstrom they would encounter at the gateway, the island of hopes and tears.

Understandably, fears on the barges greatly outweighed the hopes. Every boat horn in the harbor seemed to screech hostility, every onrushing liner or freighter seemed aimed at the small immigrant barges, every raucous voice on swiftly-moving small boats or barges seemed to explode in tormenting, insulting messages, and, in fact, many of the voices on the boats were screaming, "Go home, foreigner! Go home!"

Despair mounted, fueled by totally uninformed guesses at what the Ellis Island tests might reveal about an individual. Most of the newcomers remained grimly silent but a few argued loudly about the "correct" answers to questions, citing evidence allegedly sent to Europe by a relative or something they had read, or thought they had read. Such talk deepened the gloom.

Most of the immigrants had been up since long before dawn, donning their best clothes, many of which were esteemed in their homeland villages but would look ridiculous in the foreign land they were approaching. They counted and re-counted the tiny sums of money in pouches on strings around their necks. They checked and re-checked their entry documents. They quizzed one another, frantically hoping that they knew definite answers to questions that might be asked by immigrant officials.

Then, their small craft bumped into the Ellis Island dock. The gangplank thumped down and shouting authorities ordered the newcomers to get onto the island as soon as possible. Anxious immigrants pushed from behind, forcing the men, women, and children in front to race across the pier toward the unknown.

That passage of immigrants into the unknown went on day after day, week after week. Through sunlight and rainstorms, through fog and snow, the little ferries chugged between the ships and the island. On any normal day, 5,000 people would troop down the gangplanks and onto the island. On one incredible day, April 11, 1907, an all-time record 11,745 immigrants stepped ashore on the island. At times several ships jammed with a total of as many as 20,000 immigrants lay at anchor in the harbor, waiting to unload their human cargo. Immigrants often spent an extra day, or even several days, aboard a steamship before Ellis Island craft bore them away.

The awesome and constant surge of hopeful immigrants began peaking in 1906, when commissioner Robert Watchorn and his staff were so harassed that the commissioner considered hiring barges to house the foreigners who had to be held overnight or longer. In 1907, when 195,540 were detained, he was using "every available bit of space at the entire station." It was often stated that immigrants believed island conditions were worse than steerage. A particular need was greater refrigeration capacity: in 1907, barely one day's supply of food could be kept on the island.

The first sight and the sounds of some of the 700 uniformed island officials offered little hope to the newcomers. They wore what looked suspiciously like army uniforms. To many Europeans, any army presence was cause for dread; for those who had fled from Russian pogroms the sight evoked nearly overwhelming fear. The guides often raised their voices to be heard above the din of thousands of confused, loud-talking immigrants. Many of the uniformed personnel growled brusquely or swore profanely at the newcomers, just like soldiers back home.

Sufficient evidence exists that many of the island personnel were rude. They were mostly political appointments, not necessarily chosen because of their intelligence and more likely to be appointed for their political affiliations than for their skills in dealing with frightened people. Many cases of soliciting bribes from immigrants or harassment of females were reported, accepted, and filed. The severity of the offenses would depend directly on the standards of whomever was appointed to run the immigration center.

Most immigrants recalled being herded along by guards shouting in many languages: "Move, stupid. Hurry up. Don't dawdle." There were those who recall being insulted, as if they were animals without sensitivity. The military-style movement was not surprising. It was the job of these greeters to get this frightened, confused, anguished mass of humanity from the dock to the entrance and on to the outside world as soon as possible.

Island personnel argued that at times the unceasing pressure caused breakdowns in spirit and in courtesy. The island staff often worked 12 hours a day, in an era when overtime was only an idealistic dream. Each immigrant presented a challenge, as excited, uninformed individuals often do within mobs of anxious people.

If ever the discordant sounds of the biblical Babel were repeated on earth, it was at Ellis Island, day after day, hour after hour. The masses of foreigners comprised a wide range of nationalities— Italians, Polish, Russians, Greeks, Croats, Bulgarians, Armenians, Hungarians, Slovaks, Germans, English, Irish, Scottish, Norwegians, Swedish, and many other countries, all speaking in many tongues and varying dialects.

They asked questions or gave answers in their languages, ever raising their voices to be heard above the din. The attendants sought to shout answers in as many languages as they knew.

Few immigrants looked alike or wore the same clothing, although women of nearly every country wore brightly-hued babushkas. Many of the women and children looked stout; experienced immigrant watchers knew they were wearing as much clothing as possible—extra dresses, petticoats, and coats. Eastern Europeans with bristly mustaches and scowling expressions looked fierce. Hats of varying sizes and materials on males were about as common as the babushkas. There were Russians in fur coats and hats, even in summer, and Greeks in white kilts, even in winter weather.

The lines inched forward in groups of 30, keyed to the manifest of the ship that had brought them to America. Each immigrant was handed numbered labels that carried their number on the manifest. The 30 people moved as a unit toward the steps inside the reception building. They would wear that number until final decisions were made by the admissions staff. Each group member jostled one another, vying for position as they passed through the entrance into the tiled corridors.

The foreigners would get little more than a glance at the first floor, where their baggage had been sent. Later, those approved to leave the island would return to the first floor to buy their railroad tickets, exchange money, and buy food at sales counters. A waiting room accommodated those traveling by train beyond New York City.

At the foot of the stairs, children being carried who appeared to be more than two years old were lifted from a mother's arms and made to walk up the stairs with the adults. On those stairs, unknown to the ever-moving crowds, the first decisions on fitness for admission would be made by inspectors.

A person limping or obviously short of breath was likely to be hauled out of line at the top of the stairs as a possible victim of heart trouble. Anyone looking carefully down at the steps could be conceived to have eye trouble; he would join those taken from the line. A teenager who shuffled and stared blankly might be pulled from the line as possibly being feeble-minded. The stairs came to be known as "the six second exam."

At the top of the stairs, everyone paused, to catch their breath or merely to gasp in amazement at the Registry Room they were entering. None of them ever had seen anything so grand; for that matter, neither had most Americans. The hall was 200 feet long, 100 feet wide, with a ceiling 56 feet above the floor. There was no time to stand in admiration; uniformed personnel continued to shout in several languages: "Keep going! Move! Don't stand!"

The Registry Room was divided into several single lanes by long pipe railings, an effective means of getting the surging horde to proceed in orderly fashion. At the end of some of the lanes, each about 25 feet long, a doctor, dressed in the blue uniform of the United States Health Service, carefully watched each person as he or she walked toward him, seeking hints of each person's physical or mental fitness. The doctor's eyes would focus on the tilt of the head, the face, the scalp, the firmness of the neck, the ease of bodily motion, the gait, and general appearance, physical and mental.

That examination depended on good eyesight and medical experience, blended with common sense and often, perhaps too often, a sixth sense. In 1917, Dr. E.H. Mullen, a surgeon and United States Public Health official, discussed the matter of sixth sense:

> It occasionally happens that the inspecting officer, thinking that an approaching alien is of a certain race brings him to a standstill and questions him. The alien's facial expression and manner are peculiar and just as the officer is about to decide that this alien is mentally unbalanced, he finds that the alien in question belongs to a different race.
>
> The peculiar attitude of the alien in question is no longer peculiar; it is readily accounted for by racial considerations. Accordingly, the officer passes him on as a mentally normal person.

As each immigrant paused in front of the doctor, he intently looked at the individual's hair, face, neck, and hands. If the alien was wearing a high collar, the doctor asked that it be unbuttoned in case it were used to hide a goiter or tumor. Hats had to be removed to permit examination of the scalp for favus, a serious scalp disorder, or ringworm. The doctors asked short questions to test mental alertness. Children were asked their first names to demonstrate their mental abilities. As the line passed the doctor, he occasionally used a soft chalk to place a mark on the back of anyone suspected of physical illness or mental problems.

The doctors worked rapidly. Most of the immigrants—about 80 percent of them—passed through unmarked. But the one in every five who failed the hasty examinations was identified with a chalked letter.

The chalk marks were coded—B for back, C for conjunctivitis, Ct for trachoma, E for eyes, F for face, Ft for feet, H for heart, K for hernia, L for lameness, N for neck, P for physical and lungs, Pg for pregnancy, S for senility, Sc for scalp, X for mental retardation, and a circled K for insanity.

Anyone chalk-marked was pulled out of line and directed to a waiting area. The process was rushed, impersonal, sometimes unkind, mostly empirical, and often, wrong. But with hundreds more for each doctor to examine on any given day, it was probably as good as possible in that era.

Immediately ahead for all immigrants lay the most dreaded test of all, the examination of the eyes for trachoma or other eye diseases. No subject was more widely discussed and debated on the voyage to America than the eye test and no person was more dreaded than "the eye man." Shipboard rumors said that the test for trachoma was painful almost beyond bearing.

The lines moved, a bit slowed by trepidation, toward one of the "eye men." He tilted each immigrant's head back slightly, rolled the lid upward over a small instrument (really only an old-fashioned hook for buttoning gloves). He looked for a trace of the inflammation known as trachoma, a coating on the inner lid. Nearly all persons passed, unmarked.

Trachoma meant automatic deportation. The disease ultimately caused blindness and was incurable. Since trachoma was virtually non-existent in this country (as it still is) no steerage person afflicted with trachoma was permitted to enter the United States.

A book of instructions for the Ellis Island doctors warned that trachoma was most prevalent among "Syrians, Greeks, Armenians, Russians and Finns, and that, among the latter mentioned race, many cases of trachoma are found which give no outward evidence of the disease."

The manual also explained that the purpose of excluding the immigrants who were found to have trachoma was "not only to prevent the introduction into this country of a communicable disease, but also to keep out a class of persons from whom so large a proportion of the inmates of institutions of the blind and recipients of dispensary charity are recruited."

After the eye examination, immigrants who failed any of the preliminary physical tests faced a search of women (by a female doctor) for prostitutes, all of whom had to return to Europe. Edward A. Steiner, a minister who spent much time among steerage passengers, both aboard ships and at Ellis Island, wrote of "eight or ten women [prostitutes] marked for deportation." Steiner described them:

> They are gaily attired and betray at a glance that they belong to the guild of the daughters of the street. They claim to have come to America for all sorts of purposes, but they were caught with the men who imported them, members of a firm whose business it is to supply the New York market

> with human flesh. They know neither shame nor remorse; it is all crushed out of them.

Immigrants who escaped the chalking and the other examinations were directed back toward the main part of the Registry Hall. The chalked people were herded into detention pens, areas enclosed with wire screens. Their chance to become Americans had to be delayed, and perhaps ended forever.

Those who had passed the first mass physical examinations now faced what most of them dreaded most: the verbal examination of their fitness to become Americans. This, rather than rejection for physical reasons, had been most talked about on the ship, much of the time on the short ride from ship to the island, and now, once again discussed as they awaited the actual examination.

There was general agreement that it was best to stick with brief answers and a polite "Yes Sir" or "No Sir." That way, a person could not be confused by wondering what answer he or she had given to a previous question. It was widely believed that the verbal test would be conducted by shrewd lawyers eager to trip up an applicant.

In the end, it was not at all like what had been anticipated. Most immigrants spent less than two hours in the entire examination process. The dreaded final verbal testing generally took about two minutes and was essentially the same as the 29 questions tendered in Europe at the point of embarkation. The immigrant who was detained longer almost always was the victim of his own terror that could bring on memory lapses.

After a wait of about an hour, even on the busiest days, immigrants would be aligned in groups of 30, with numbers conforming to the ship's manifest entries, the guideline through their entire steerage and Ellis Island experiences. They would be led, by number, to meet with one of the interrogators. To help ease the tension, instructional information was posted in at least nine common languages and interpreters were available for almost every language. But many of the foreign hopefuls were so distraught that they could not think or read even in their own languages. For many, even the first question might be difficult: "What is your name?"

Helen Barth, who worked at Ellis Island for the Hebrew Immigrant Aid Society from 1914 to 1917, wrote of that: "The inspector would say, 'Where do you come from?' and they would say 'Berlin.' The inspector would put down the name 'Berliner.' The name was not Berliner. That is no name.

Myerson could become Meyers. In similar fashion, many other names ending with son, such as Abrahamson, were shortened to Abraham. Names ending with "smith," as in Goldsmith, were shortened to Gold. Goldenburger could become Golden. A long Polish name such as Skyzertski, might be so difficult to spell that the inspector would merely write "Skies" or "Sanda." One Ellis Island story told of the befuddled, fearful German Jew who, when asked his name, answered, "Ich vergessin" (I forget). He left the island as "Ike Ferguson" and remained that for all his life.

An inspector might even suggest a new spelling and occasionally a callous inspector might change the name in what he considered a huge joke, or possibly as another slur covertly aimed at the anxious foreigners. The awed newcomers almost always were too overwhelmed to protest name changes or even, at times, to understand what was going on.

After that, for most of the way, the questions were simple—age, marital status, occupation, ability to read and write, nationality, last permanent residence. Then, they came increasingly to the point: Where are you now? Where are you going? Do you have a ticket? Did you pay for your passage over, or who did pay? Do you have money with you? How much? It was believed that $25 was the proper answer. Are you going to join a relative? What is his name and where does he live?

Inspectors might expand various questions if they thought there was a need to delve further. Among the tales preserved in the comprehensive Ellis Island archives, there is the brief story of a young woman who was asked, "Would you wash stairs from the top down or the bottom up?" She responded tartly: "I did not come to America to wash stairs."

Eventually the questioning reached the ambiguous query that troubled nearly all immigrants: "Are you under contract, expressed or implied, to perform labor in the United States? A "yes" answer was absolutely wrong—and against the law that forbade contract labor. A "no" answer, while not illegal, could cause closer questioning to determine whether the individual might become a ward of the state. An acceptable answer was an expressed note of optimism: "I hope to get work in the United States."

Beyond that it was easy, unless the answer had to be yes: Have you ever been in prison, in a warehouse, or supported by charity? Are you a polygamist (or a prostitute or an anarchist)?

Virtually all immigrants believed that they must have $25 or more to enter the United States. The sum was freely mentioned by those seeking to get Europeans to leave their homes—the steamship companies, the railroad agencies, articles in their homeland newspapers, and in letters sent back to those still living in European areas. Ship's officers who filled out the manifests in Europe asked about money. The inference was clear: have money or you do not get in.

William Williams, the commissioner of immigration appointed by President Roosevelt, was a stout opponent of what he called "low grade immigrants" (all those other than Anglo-Saxons). In 1910 he instituted a rule that required immigrants to have $10 each and tickets to their ultimate destinations if they were traveling beyond New York. His successor, Robert Watchorn, repealed the $10 provision, but Williams regained the office four years later and promptly reinstated the minimum money rule—and upped the ante to $25.

Although the $25 regulation was soon repealed, inspectors continued to retain that "means test" for many years. It was a genuine hardship: $25 was considerably more than American laborers made in a month. Immigrants who sent money home to bring wives and children or other relatives to America strove to save $1 a week. At that rate it took nearly half a year to save $25.

The immigrant was not without friends on Ellis Island. Interpreters for many languages were available and religious and national societies were on the island to help immigrants. They would be close during the entire examination process and continue to help as the accepted immigrants moved toward the money exchange, railroad tickets, and reunions with relatives or friends who had come to the island take them home.

The possibility that an unaccompanied woman might be sold into "white slavery" (as prostitution was quaintly known in the nineteenth century) made it extremely difficult for women traveling alone. They would be held on the island until an expected male arrived or until one of the social agencies guaranteed to take care of her in America. If such help never came, the helpless female was assigned to a pen with others to await deportation.

Candidates for admission to the United States could be turned back if they admitted to being criminals in the old world, or if they were thought to be polygamists, anarchists, or those shown by testing to be illiterate or mentally disturbed.

Women immigrants faced unique hardships on the island, just as they had in steerage. There were always the male employees who saw a woman as a potential sex partner—and made overtures suggesting that compliance with an inspector's hint of a later meeting in a New York hotel would hasten admittance to America.

Numerous young women who arrived at Ellis Island with all arrangements in place to marry a special friend or fiance in America were treated with respect and given special attention—providing that the special friend appeared at the island.

Frank Martucci, who began working as an inspector in 1907, said that he had lost count but was sure he had helped in "hundreds and hundreds of weddings of all nationalities and all types." In time, the weddings were performed at City Hall in New York. Martucci described the Ellis Island weddings:

> Incidentally, you may have heard, there is a post at Ellis Island which through long usage has come to earn the name of "The Kissing Post." It is probably the spot of greatest interest on the island, and if the immigrants recall it afterward it is always, I am sure, with fondness. For myself, I found it a real joy to watch some of the tender scenes that took place there.
>
> There was a line of desks where the inspectors stood with their backs toward the windows and facing the wall. Further back behind a partition, the witnesses (friends and relatives) waited outside for the detained aliens. As the aliens were brought out, the witnesses were brought in to be examined as to their rights of claim. If the inspector found no hitch, they were allowed to join each other. This, because of the arrangement of the partition, usually took place at "The Kissing Post," where friends, sweethearts, husbands and wives, parents and children would embrace and kiss and shed tears of real joy.

Martucci's romantic version of the marriages was in sharp contrast to the very intense problems on Ellis Island. There was some justification for the extra attention paid single women; they could not be let out on the streets of New York without the possibility of major harm. Thus a single woman underwent severe questioning about her single status, where she was going, who would meet her, how much money she had, and whether her passage had been paid by herself or by a charitable organization. The same standards prevailed for children traveling with a mother who had not yet been contacted by a husband already in America.

Edward Corsi, an inspector on Ellis Island since 1907, told of a particularly dreadful episode on the island for detained females (who were kept in a wire-enclosed area called "The Pen"):

> One Sunday morning, I remember, there were seventeen hundred of these women and children packed in one room with a normal capacity of six hundred. . . .
>
> Sometimes these women were placed in the hands of a social agency which promised to be responsible to the Commissioner, caring for them or placing them in some appropriate employment. But if everything had been done, and the missing husband or fiance could not be found, the poor alien, despite all her tears, had to be returned to her native country.

The distress of those who were detained for possible deportation naturally cast a pall over the jubilation and the joy in passing all tests and being admitted. As previously stated, about 20 percent of all immigrants went through special physical and mental examinations. Nearly all of them were quickly cleared to join their friends and relatives in the verbal examination lines.

After the testing and the examination, entrance into the United States was surprisingly easy. Immigrants required no special papers or proof of clearance at Ellis Island. Passports were not required until 1921. The newcomers eventually had to secure naturalization papers as proof of citizenship.

But the deportation pens received what amounted over the years to about 2 percent of all immigrants. While that seems like a very small percentage, 2 percent of the total of about 15 million persons who went through Ellis Island between 1892 and 1915 amounted to the deportation of 280,000 to 300,000 men, women, and children, enough for a small city. Their anguish was indescribable—and the perils they could face back in Europe were horrifying.

Chapter Eleven

"COMMITTING A GROSS INJUSTICE"

Deportation of immigrants to Europe was not a matter of simply returning them to the villages or cities from whence they had initially departed. There they might find friends or family. Deportation meant returning to the port from whence they had sailed for America—back to Naples or Bremerhaven, Trieste or Liverpool, Piraeus or Fiume—or any of the other major European embarking ports.

Since nearly all of the villages and cities of a deported immigrant were likely to be far distant from the point of embarkation, returning them to the port where they last saw Europe was grossly unfair and even barbaric for a nation that boasted around the world of its freedoms and spirit of justice.

Imagine, for example, the 11-year-old girl who was returned to Bremen because of trachoma. The law said that a parent had to accompany any deported child under ten. But those over that arbitrary age were sent back to Europe alone (unless a parent elected to return with the deported person) and unceremoniously released in the port from which she had sailed.

The steamship company was obligated to return her to Europe at its own expense, making her a liability in the company's profit-and-loss books. As such, she was not likely to be treated even as well as she might have been in America-bound steerage.

At the European port where the steamship company completed its contract, the child would meet criminals and degenerates eager to take charge of her life. The thought of a penniless 11-year-old girl alone on the docks of a European port (or any port in any land) was as cruel a fate as could be imagined.

It is important to consider deportation, of any individual, for almost any reason. The money-making machinery was greased to roll the lines of immigrants to America—not to take them home again. Inspecting and questioning immigrants in Europe and removing defective individuals from the ship's manifest was a logical—if slightly more expensive—way of dealing with departing Europeans. Ship companies too often ignored the obligation. It was cheaper to take a chance on an American rejection and pay the fee for returning the victim to Europe.

Commissioner of immigration Frederick Wallis, in a 1921 letter written to Washington superiors, bitterly protested against the system that encouraged people to come to America only to be told once here that they must go back. He concluded:

> I do believe our nation is committing a gross injustice for which some day it must render an account, in allowing these hundreds of thousands of people to sell all they have, sever all connections, come four thousand miles out of the heart of Europe and other countries, only to find after they have passed the Statue of Liberty that they must go back to the port from whence they came.
>
> Our Inspection and examination should be conducted on the other side, thus saving thousands of people the suffering we see at this island daily and which is indescribable and would melt a heart of granite. The last great days of assize will disclose no sadder scenes than separation is producing at this station. Examination on the other side is ten thousand times better than rejection on this side.

In most months, an average of about a thousand immigrants were deported. In the peak year, 1907, when 1,285,000 newcomers entered Ellis Island, 13,064 of them were deported, slightly more than 1 percent. In the long range, however, approximately 2 percent were deported.

About two-thirds of all deportees were persons judged likely to become public charges, which could include persons without sufficient funds or likelihood of a job, unmarried women, and those with physical imperfections that could handicap them in the United States. The second major reason for rejection was attempting to enter via fraud or improper documents.

The dreaded road to deportation began with the 20 percent who were pulled out of the first examination line in Registry Hall. Many of them were ordered to rooms for immigrants being examined for possible physical deficiencies. As preparation for a probing physical examination, the immigrants had to strip, an especially humiliating and embarrassing ordeal for modest young European women. Those held for further examination had their clothing fumigated while they endured lukewarm to cold showers.

Many of those held beyond a few hours or a day or more were young women who had come to the United States in the belief that a fiance or a husband would meet them on Ellis Island for a joyous, lovely reunion. If she were going into New York City, Brooklyn, or New Jersey to meet her loved one, the island staff had no authority to let her loose on her own in the strict Victorian mores of that period. Also retained were minors who expected someone to meet them or others who did not have money but thought someone with necessary funds would appear.

Edward Corsi, a former director of Ellis Island, recounted in his memoirs the lack of facilities for those retained because of failed reunions with relatives or guardians: We generally had more of this class than we could handle. . . . They just couldn't move about, and when we wanted to get one out it was almost a major operation.

As previously stated, nine out of ten were reunited with their families and friends in a day or less. Detained immigrants went before a three-man Board of Special Inquiry to answer questions about their right to stay in America. A rejected immigrant could appeal his or her case before the secretary of commerce and labor in Washington, and a high percentage of appeals were sustained. But for the ultimately rejected 2 percent, it had come time for the voyage of the wretched and the forgotten.

Religious and charitable organizations often protested deportations and sometimes won, but the big political anti-immigrant voices could not be overcome. There were sympathetic and conscientious staff members on the island, but they were helpless against the juggernaut of a powerful, unquestionably biased system.

Among the deported, of course, were criminals and paupers, ne'er-do-wells and polygamists, trachoma-infected and weak-minded; there were old men and women, snatched from their families because of their age, and little children taken from their parents because of physical or mental problems. Mingled with the majority of innocents were the women whose gentleman friends had failed to appear, and prostitutes whose sponsors had failed them. If all of these had been genuine ladies of the evening in an organized crime ring, their sponsors likely would have had them sent to America first or second class, where there would be no morality tests.

Deported immigrants could not be placed on the first eastbound steamship. They had to return in the steerage of a ship from the company line that had carried them to America. As a matter of economy (for the steamship company), men, women, and children had to wait as much as two or three weeks until the company that had brought them to Ellis Island loaded enough of them into the steerage of a vessel designated by the company.

The unfortunate deportees waited in rooms packed tightly with fellow victims; in one shocking night, 1,700 children slept in a dormitory with beds for 600. Adults often faced similar conditions. As they waited to go "home," they slept on filthy floors, awakened to the cries of people whose wills and minds were cracking. It is no wonder that about 3,000 persons committed suicide on Ellis Island. It was not America's shining hour.

"Committing a Gross Injustice"

Henry Curran, who became commissioner of Ellis Island in 1923, later recalled in his book *Pillar to Post* some of the intolerable conditions on the island. Although there were beds in some of the detention rooms, most detainees slept on the floor in the main hall behind wire cages. As many as 2,000 immigrants slept thus each night in bedbug-infested accommodations as federal support for immigrant handling declined.

Curran went to Washington and induced two congressmen to visit the island and its bedbugs. He said the visitors quickly sized up the disgusting situation. Curran recalled: "The wheels began to turn. Those congressmen were flaming missionaries for beds instead of cages."

The hands of Ellis Island officials were tied by the rigid immigration laws. In fairness to most of them, they sought to find the missing lovers or guardians or to find help for many others. Often the detained people were admitted through a pledge by a charitable organization that it would lend full aid if the questionable people were admitted to America. Corsi summed up the situation for the rest of them:

> The results were tragic indeed. As I know from personal experience. There was no way of soothing these heartbroken women who had traveled thousands and thousands of miles. Endured suffering and humiliation, and had uprooted their lives only to find their hopes shattered at the end of the long voyage. These, I think, are the saddest of immigrant cases.

Legally deported immigrants were by no means the only immigrants who returned to their native lands. Large numbers of those admitted in time went back to their native lands voluntarily, paying their way home for brief visits. There they extolled the virtues of America and proved it in their own prosperous appearances. But there were hundreds of thousands of men and women who, in a process called "remigration," went back home to live out their lives in the open fields and woodlands that they loved, preferring the restrictions of their old villages or cities to the confused, frenetic pace of America.

Thomas J. Archdeacon, in *Becoming American*, cited statistics that showed 3,574,974 foreigners left America voluntarily between 1908 and 1924, an annual average of 210,293. At least 30 percent of all immigrants returned to their native lands, some of them with nest eggs painfully tucked away out of meager earnings, some still with little or no money, and some with enough to bring their families to America with them when they returned to America. Such an immigrant had to go once more through the Ellis Island procedure. Most felt it was much easier the second time around.

Among the nations with large numbers of immigrants to the United States, Italians had the greatest numbers returning, possibly because they were among the foreign groups that received the harshest treatment in America. Archdeacon estimated that about 1.1 million Italians returned to their home countries in the period cited above.

Many Greeks who came to the United States in the early twentieth century did not expect to stay very long. They migrated, hoping to make money and then return to their native land. Many Greek men believed they could more quickly earn the dowry expected of them by working in the United States. Favorable working conditions prompted many to remain permanently in America, but even they usually went home to marry a Greek woman or sent money to bring her to the United States. About 54 percent of all Greeks returned to their homeland.

Chapter Twelve

THE TOUGH ROAD TO AMERICANIZATION

Immigrants who had arrived in America the easy way—by buying first- or second-class tickets—had a rude comeuppance once they left the comfort and asylum of their ships. They were in America, and they faced American chicanery on the docks of New York City and those of Hoboken and Jersey City on the New Jersey side of the Hudson River.

A three-year study released in 1914 by the New Jersey Commission of Immigration was one of the frankest and most startling studies ever made of immigrants as they entered the country. It concentrated on two New Jersey cities, Hoboken and Jersey City, where four of the nation's largest trunk railroads and four of the largest transatlantic steamship companies were located. The report began: "The sum total of their [immigrants'] assets when they enter the country are first, a good physique; second, an average of $50 in money; and third, hope. . . . Many, however, are robbed of their last two assets before they have passed beyond a New Jersey terminal."

Ellis Island officials sought in 1892 to protect all immigrants of any shipping classification by having all aliens debarked at Ellis Island. High level protests from steamship companies and the more august passengers squelched that. If the island leaders had prevailed, there would have been ample opportunity to warn all newcomers of the dangers and cheating that could be expected as soon as immigrants were on their own.

But left to the not-tender mercies of unofficial, self-appointed dockside greeters, the cabin class passengers faced cruel fleecing within sight of both Ellis Island and the Statue of Liberty. "Porters" met the ships, conspiring with hotel owners, cab drivers, and employment agencies to bilk the newcomers. Reporting that there were "no trains to the West" on any given day, they overcharged their victims for reservations in high-priced hotels and delivered railroad tickets for exorbitant prices. Baggage was "weighed" and "checked"on the docks by bogus agents; the baffled foreigners paid a fee to have it released. Unofficial threats of deportation flared on the docks; the immigrants did not dare ask questions or answer back.

Steerage passengers were, for once, fortunate. After the rigors of Ellis Island they were guided by officials to their friends and approved transportation, then taken by ferry to The Battery in New York City or to one of the railroad terminals in Hoboken or Jersey City. The luckiest of all, as far as leaving the island was concerned, were those bound for the city, including those who would board trains for upstate New York or New England. These newcomers walked down the final Ellis Island corridor to doors where a sign said, "Push. To New York." Beyond the door, friends and relatives were frantically waving.

The sounds of welcome enriched the landing at The Battery in New York City. Top-heavy piles of luggage were loaded into horse-drawn wagons that made the rounds of the addresses on the labels. City-wise friends advised the new arrivals to get rid of their "foreign" clothing, lest they be laughed at in the neighborhood. Ann Novotny caught the flavor in *Strangers at the Door*:

> Half an hour after the ferry had unloaded a fresh crop of immigrants, the public dressing rooms and even the sidewalks around the park were littered with abandoned kerchiefs, visored caps, and occasional shirts and trousers. So the citizens-to-be set off into the New World, marveling at the tall buildings, the clean-shaven men, the first small black children, or an amazing automobile, while their friends laughed about their astonishment.

There would be partying in a friend's flat, with loud talk and some home cooking in one of the ghetto apartments where immigrants clustered in areas divided by nationality. The newcomers might be curious about a sewing machine or two or piles of unfinished garments in a corner of the host's cramped living space, but they laid their questions aside, took a luxurious bath, and slept, untroubled by what would happen tomorrow.

Some went uptown the next morning to the Grand Central Station to head north toward the factories near Albany or northeast to the mills of Providence, Rhode Island; and Boston or Lowell, Massachusetts. They willingly accepted low paying jobs, believing that soon the financial largess of America and the kindness of its people must soon come their way.

Ferries that took immigrants to railroad terminals in Jersey City and Hoboken in New Jersey disgorged the foreigners on cement platforms open to snow, rain, and New Jersey's piercing summertime sun. Hundreds of them might wait for hours while their trains backed into the stations. They clutched their tickets and edged forward to board the aging cars that the railroads used on most immigrant trains.

The Tough Road to Americanization

The westbound trains stopped often—in highly multi-ethnic and diversified Newark, New Jersey, and at depots near Passaic's woolen mills or Paterson's silk and heavy machine works. On and on rolled the trains, to the iron mines in northwest New Jersey and the anthracite coal mines in eastern Pennsylvania. The trains stopped in every industrial city—Pittsburgh, Toledo, Detroit, Cincinnati, Chicago, and went beyond to the wheat fields of the American plains. In Chicago, immigrants hoped for work in the railroad yards and slaughterhouses and became the "shoulders"of the city that Carl Sandburg extolled in his writings. In Chicago, too, they could transfer to trains bound for places as far west as San Francisco.

Those immigrants gave the cities and towns their greatest need: the strong backs of people willing and able to undertake the dangerous mining and the daunting jobs in the steel mills and the menial, underpaid tasks in thousands of factories. They double-tracked the railroads, paved the city streets, carried cement and bricks up ladders to build skyscrapers, and fashioned the towering city cathedrals in which the Catholic immigrants reposed their faith. They labored on the great spans that carried trains and automobiles over the rivers, and sweated in the tunnels that took railroads under the rivers.

Wherever they worked, nearly all immigrants were at the bottom of the ladder in every way—in pay, the chance to advance, and respect from bosses. Most found employment in low-status, manual labor jobs in factories, mines, and construction, and as self-employed piece workers in their city flats.

It was common for immigrants to work an 84-hour work week (14 hours per day, six days a week). Jobs offered no paid vacations, sick pay, medical help, or pension plans. Dingy, dirty, unventilated, hot in summer and cold and drafty in winter, the factories could be death traps. Workers often became entangled in the uncovered, dangerous moving parts of machinery. At worst, a fire could snuff out dozens of lives. Pay was shockingly low; few workers in America had ever been as exploited by the captains of industry as were these southern and eastern Europeans. Average pay was about $400 a year for a male, lower for females, and much lower for children. It was virtually impossible to escape from the ravages of poverty.

Immigrants tended to gather together in their own "Little Italy," "Little Dublin," "Little Poland," "Little Russia," "Little Hungary," and so on. They centered their activities initially in their Catholic churches and Jewish synagogues, for there they found the familiar comforts and beloved tongues of old and the desperately needed reassurance of their own worth.

A major example of immigrants moving heavily into neighborhoods of people from their own homelands was the Polish section of Chicago, centered on St.

Stanislaus Kostka Church. That house of worship deftly blended staunch Roman Catholicism, Polish culture, and a full range of services vitally needed by the immigrants. By 1899, Stanislaus Kostka Church was known as the world's largest Catholic parish.

Somewhat strangely, most of the southern and eastern Europeans who had been farmers in the old country streamed into the cities of America on the plausible theory that work was there. They crowded into miserable, cold-water flats in New York City and into shanties on the edges of most cities and large towns. Wretched though their homeland dwellings might have been, these foreigners could be excused for feeling they had made no progress at all.

Considerable numbers of Italians ventured into the countryside surrounding New York City to work on the handsome estates that millionaires built within railroad commuting distance of the city's banks, insurance companies, and the stock market. The immigrants very seldom lived on the great estates, but rather gathered together in nearby small towns to live on patches of ground that always featured as big a vegetable garden as possible.

These immigrants labored to secure a precarious foothold, taking almost any job. They set up shop in their dark little apartments, finishing garments at a low piece work rate. The whole family worked at the sewing machines in "sweatshops" that evaded city laws that required licenses. Often they worked 15 to 18 hours a day just to stay even.

The contributions of immigrant workers cannot be minimized, but neither can their work be glorified, unless working the longest hours at the hardest jobs and receiving the lowest pay deserves glorification. Their lives for the most part were drudgery verging on low-paid slavery. Little children worked in the sweatshops: numerous accounts were published of eight-year-old girls with "pale serious faces" and "stooped shoulders" in textile mills or six- to eight-year-old sad-eyed, weary boys laboring in coal mines or glass factories.

Employers used immigrants for the dirtiest, most detestable jobs, like inexpensive, uncomplaining machines that could be thrown out when defective or worn out. Labor unions saw them as unfair competition, willing to work for cut-rate wages. It was not uncommon for road contractors of 1900, mostly descendants of the first Irish newcomers, to advertise for "25 Italians or one Irishman." Frank Julian Warne, in a smug study of immigrants published in 1916, bluntly declared: "That they have many virtues there is no denying; still they simply are rough, unskilled, illiterate, unimaginative, hard-working laborers, and even in America, with all its opportunities, they will never be anything else."

Warne was wrong, for bigotry has no claim to foresight, but in 1916 he had legions of believers. An immigrant was fair game for everyone, including, far too often, fellow countrymen who had preceded him to America by a few years or only a few months.

Hastily organized foreign "banks" in every state and nearly every city became social and business centers for immigrants. According to the 1914 New Jersey study of immigrants, the banker was a man who did "practically any task which might be demanded of him by his more ignorant neighbors, not the least of which is the safeguarding of their money and sending it abroad."

New Jersey in 1912 had seven Italian, five Hungarian, one Polish, and one German bank, plus sixteen Italian and nine Hungarian "money transmitters." An astonishing total of $13 million was sent abroad annually by New Jersey immigrants.

For every authorized banker or transmitter, the report said, there were often six unauthorized operators. Fraud was rampant. One unauthorized "bank" had no passbooks but instead issued promissory notes to depositors. That "banker's" greed got the better part of him when he made his depositors sign the notes, which he then discounted in a legitimate bank. When his "bank" collapsed, the depositors not only had lost their money but owed payments on the promissory notes as well.

The New Jersey Commission report on Immigration in 1914 listed other exploiters: justices of the peace, notaries public, employment agencies, and self-appointed neighborhood leaders. In 1912, eight foreign consulates refused to accept any document sworn to by a New Jersey notary public. "Employment agencies" charged heavy fees, bullied workers, and often sent immigrants traveling far on railroads to non-existent jobs.

Yet immigrants persevered, seeking solace in city and town neighborhoods that were predominantly from their own homeland or even their home towns or cities in Europe. As soon as possible they formed a neighborhood church or temple. Often these began in the basements of existing churches, then grew to create new foreign-speaking parishes.

Americans often complained that the newer immigrants tended to "stick together too much." That was true, of course, and logical since these new arrivals needed someone with whom they could speak in their native tongues. It was also true of earlier large-scale immigrants: the early Irish newcomers had also lived close to their Catholic churches and Germans chose to be close to their churches, rathskellers, and turner halls.

"Sticking together" for nearly all immigrants was usually a matter of finding living quarters within their meager grasps. Studies in Chicago in the early years of the twentieth century showed that they tended to live in multi-story wooden tenements with little heat, little ventilation, and no bathrooms. Many shared the one toilet allotted to each floor. Two or more families commonly shared a four-room apartment.

At about the same time, New York immigrants mainly lived in tall tenements. Immigrants usually occupied three or four rooms at an average rent of $4 per room each month. Germans and the Irish were moving out as Italians and Jews moved in. Heat came from small coal stoves, fueled by coal bought on the streets at 10¢ for 25 pounds. Adults and older boys used public baths for cleanliness; small children bathed weekly in a tin tub beside the kitchen stove.

The tenement hovels and the noisy, pulsating sounds of street peddlars were reminiscent of the worst of the London slums so vividly portrayed in the nineteenth-century novels of Charles Dickens. Fist fighting among rival gangs and thievery on the streets near public entertainments were common. Sickness was rife and doctors were scarce. Summer brought torturous nights, when tenement dwellers slept on narrow balconies or on the flat roofs of their buildings.

Throughout every major wave of immigration there arose consistent animosity against the newest people who forsook steerage for a permanent lifestyle. The first great wave of Irish Catholics irritated America's predominantly Protestant culture in the 1840s. Germans who arrived after the Fatherland's revolution in 1848 stirred fears that their intellectualism and revolutionary spirit might destroy old values. The swarms of foreigners who swept into the nation after 1875 alarmed American labor unions. The greatest animosity was directed at Jews. They often were caricatured as money-grubbing Shylocks, a cruelly unjust view of Jewish immigrants who toiled at piecework in their city flats.

Labor unions feared that the multi-religious, poorly-educated southern and eastern Europeans who swarmed into Ellis Island after 1890 would work for pittances and thus undermine the hard-won wage standards of union members. Law enforcement agents believed these swarthy, uneducated, and poor immigrants would create uncontrollable social disturbances in the cities. Many urban and suburban officials feared that these people, largely peasants in Europe, would overwhelm the relief agencies of America.

Anne Novotny in *Strangers at the Door* effectively summed up the plight of immigrant workers in the late nineteenth-century American system of building great fortunes on the backs of the poor in the slaughterhouses and meat packing plants of Chicago, the dark and perilous steel mills of Youngstown, the steel mills of Pittsburgh, and the textile plants of Fall River, where an 84-hour week was not uncommon.

Exploitation was rampant and perhaps no group was more exploited than the Greek shoeshine boys. A New Jersey study found them in most major cities, where they worked a minimum of 15 hours daily, seven days a week. Their exploiters, older fellow immigrants, took all tips, fed their unofficial slaves greasy food, gave them dirty beds in overcrowded rooms, and rewarded them with about $15 a month. The average boy netted his "sponsor" about $300 to $500 a year. Yet most boys saved enough to send tiny amounts home to Greece.

Emily Greene Balch, a Wellesley professor not given to mitigating the plight of immigrants, saw a bright side in her 1910 book *Our Slavic Fellow Citizens*: "From a purely aesthetic point of view, no one need wish for a prettier sight than a Passaic handkerchief factory full of Polish girls in kerchiefs of pale yellow and other soft colors, the afternoon sun slanting across the fine stuff on which they are working."

Miss Balch's poetic awareness of the Polish handkerchief girls led her to praise the neatness of Slavic homes and the penchant of Slavic women to decorate their rooms, to the extent that "the gods of the Slavic house are orderliness and decoration." She did not allow herself to be blinded by virtue. The Slav, like all immigrants, did not dissolve easily into the so-called melting pot. What Miss Balch wrote of the Slovak might fit all of the newly arrived:

> The immigrant sees less of America than we think. He comes over with the Slovaks, goes to a Slovak boarding house, a Slovak store, a Slovak saloon and a Slovak bank. His boss is likely a Slovak. He deals with Americans only as the street car conductor shouts, "What do you want, John?" or when boys stone his children and call them "Hunkies."

The "new immigrants" quite naturally sought to maintain their traditions, as had the Irish, the Germans, and other Anglo-Saxons of an earlier day. Yet these hard-working, over-stressed newcomers from southern and eastern Europe recognized that success lay in moving toward the mainstream.

They had plenty of help from established American sources, which ranged from the Daughters of the American Revolution to women's clubs, church leaders, and earlier immigrants from their home countries or regions. The primary emphasis at first was to teach "Americanization," but that soon flowed into much broader and sounder emphasis on life skills. Especially helpful were settlement houses (also known as neighborhood houses), built by subscriptions from the Anglo-Saxon communities and maintained by volunteers.

The new immigrants accepted the philosophy that education was the fastest and surest way out of their deplorable situations. Somehow, as described in many diaries or letters, many adults managed to attend night schools to learn the English language that their bosses spoke.

Encouraged by sympathetic teachers in both the public and parochial schools, children of immigrants began attending elementary schools. Their progress was slow by modern standards, but most of them finished at least five or six grades before going to work—not a reflection on the immigrants because as the twentieth century began, a fifth or sixth grade education was normal for nearly all students.

Education was a major factor in easing foreigners into the mainstream, but the playgrounds also exerted a strong influence. Boys learned to play American sports, particularly baseball, and girls learned such games as hopscotch and the rhythmic chants of jumping rope.

Churches, particularly the Catholic churches, exerted a strong influence in keeping their members within the law. Free public libraries, something unknown in the old countries, urged children to take books home—in some cases to bring books to their parents published in a familiar homeland language.

The children of immigrants began to believe in themselves and their place in American society. Americans liked the immigrants' spaghetti, their bagels, their noodles, their goulash, their confections. Young men and women increasingly enjoyed the dances that immigrants had introduced. Powerful muscles proved as useful on the football and baseball fields as in the clay pits and coal mines. World War I hastened the assimilation, since enlistment earned citizenship.

The problems, the exploitations, the animosities, the misunderstandings, and the smouldering hatreds would continue, but by the 1920s they were lessening. The process was slow, but at least it continued. By the end of World War II the grandsons and granddaughters of the new immigrants were attending college and assuming the role of equality that had been promised by the laws of the United States of America.

Chapter Thirteen

CLOSING THE GOLDEN DOOR

As the clouds of war thickened across Europe in 1914, huge numbers of immigrants continued to flow westward into Ellis Island. The onrushing war had little effect in 1914, when a total of 878,052 immigrants passed through the doors and into America, an average of about 3,000 a day. A year later, as the war became a brutal bloodbath, the total of persons passing through Ellis Island dropped to 178,416, slightly less than 600 each day.

In 1914, President Woodrow Wilson appointed a personal friend, law professor Frederick Howe, as island administrator. Howe immediately instituted sweeping humanistic changes based on his philosophy that he and the staff must seek to "imagine what a detained immigrant must be feeling." Howe permitted immigrants to get fresh air on the island lawns and provided entertainment. His concern for the newcomers brought a storm of criticism that immigrants were being coddled.

Wilson ordered in 1915 that no aliens be deported during the war; sending them home to villages or cities that might no longer exist would have been cruelty beyond reckoning. When the United States declared war in 1917, about 1,150 seamen on German and Austrian ships were captured and sent to Ellis Island. (They later were sent to camps in Georgia and North Carolina.) Early in 1918, the Army Medical Department took over the Ellis Island Hospital and during the war the navy quartered on the island men who were awaiting permanent assignments.

Propaganda against southern and eastern Europeans intensified as World War I expanded. Madison Grant, an anthropologist at the National Museum of Natural History, in his popular book *The Passing of the Great Race*, claimed that President Abraham Lincoln's Emancipation Proclamation had created an aura that eventually led to "the intrusion of immigrants of inferior racial value." The result, Grant alleged, was that European governments unloaded on "careless, wealthy and hospitable America the sweepings of their jails and asylums."

Congress jumped on the careening anti-immigrant bandwagon early in 1917, passing a law that listed 33 reasons to turn back immigrants. Most contentious was a clause excluding immigrants over 16 years of age who could not read 30 or 40 test words in their own language or dialect. President Wilson vetoed the law,

Congress overrode the veto, and the exclusionary provision remained on the books until 1952.

Fears of Communists and anarchists swept the nation in 1919. About 2,500 alleged "revolutionists" were rounded up and sent to Ellis Island to await deportation. Several hundred of them were returned to Europe after brief, perfunctory hearings where the decisions were in place before the trials began.

Commissioner Howe complained that he had become a jailer to men who had not been convicted of any crime:

> They were brought under guards and on special trains with instructions to get them away from the country with as little delay as possible. Most of the aliens had been picked up in raids on labor headquarters. . . .
>
> In these proceedings, the inspector who had made the arrest was prosecutor, witness, judge, jailer and executioner. He was clerk and interpreter as well. This was all the trial that the alien could demand.

On January 4, 1920, the *New York Times* declared: "With 500 foreign-born members of the Communist Party on Ellis Island and more than 2,500 others held elsewhere for deportation, the torch of the Red revolution in America burned low last night." By then, the "Red Scare" was diminishing to the point of being non-existent.

Immigrant arrivals dropped sharply in 1918, when 28,867 foreigners cleared the island, and in 1919, when the total was a mere 26,731 (a daily average of about 90). Most staff members either quit or were fired as work on the island diminished.

Anti-immigrant feelings soared as the early 1920s progressed. Surprisingly, however, 560,971 immigrants entered America through Ellis Island in 1921. The facility desperately needed repairs, the staff was inexperienced, and the required test for literacy considerably slowed the entrance process. Worse, many on the staff had reverted to the old island practices of deceit and dishonesty, gouging immigrants for money or favors as often as possible.

Forty doctors each sought to examine 100 immigrants each day, and the new requirements made it impossible to check more than 20 thoroughly. Through the spring and summer of 1920, about 5,000 immigrants arrived in New York Harbor daily. Because of the backlog of people already on the island, steamships anchored in the harbor were forced to keep steerage passengers for hours, even days, until space could be found on the island.

Newspapers made much of the wretched conditions at Ellis Island—dirty baths and toilets, a shortage of beds, dormitories filled with lice and other vermin, and an underpaid, overwhelmed staff. The island well deserved its common nickname, "the cattle farm."

Congress reacted to the mounting feeling across the nation that immigrants must be limited. As strict quota laws began to be enforced, thousands of men, women, and children were stranded on Ellis Island awaiting their fates. Henry Curran, a New York Republican politician, took charge of the island on July 1, 1923. On his first day, he reported that he found 2,000 men, women, and children listed on the island as "excess quota." In his book of remembrances, *Pillar to Post*, published in 1941, he wrote an eloquent, sorrow-tinged account:

> In a week or two they all went back. I was powerless. I could only watch them go. Day by day the barges took them from Ellis island back to the ships again, back to what? As they trooped aboard the big barges under my window, carrying their heavy bundles, some in the quaint, colorful native costumes worn to celebrate their first day in free America, some carrying little American flags, most of them quietly weeping, they twisted something in my heart that hurts to this day.

From an immigrant standpoint, an even more hurtful blow came in May 1924, when Congress enacted a quota law whose chief purpose was to satisfy those ranting that immigrants from southern and eastern Europe were diluting and polluting the American image. The new regulation limited annual immigration to 2 percent of a sending nation's population in the United States as of the 1890 census.

The words "eliminating southern and eastern Europeans" did not appear in the legislation, but the effect was fiendishly effective in doing that. Northern and western Europeans were heavily favored—the Anglo-Saxon immigrants in 1890 totaled 87.6 percent of the United States population. It did not take a mathematical genius to arrive at the figure for southern and eastern Europeans—12.4 percent.

Those restrictive, patently unfair quotas remained on the books through World War II and beyond. Nearly three decades later, United States President Harry Truman, never one for softening a criticism, bluntly—and quite accurately—said, "The idea behind this discriminatory policy was, to put it boldly, that Americans with English and Irish names were better people and better citizens than Americans with Italian or Greek or Polish names."

In another restrictive provision, the new law required that potential immigrants must be inspected in American consulates overseas. If they passed, they would be given a visa in their countries of origin before moving westward to America.

The overall ceiling on immigrants was cut to 164,000 people a year (from 358,000 in 1923.) Italy's quota was cut from 42,057 a year to 3,845. The commissioner general of immigration commented on, and lamented, the 1924 changes:

> Prior to 1924, when the last quota law was enacted, the bulk of immigrants poured through our seaports. Ellis Island, New York,was the great portal—the gateway through which an immigrant entered the land of opportunity. The land border ports were of secondary significance.
>
> If the expressions "Ellis Island" and "Immigration" were not synonymous, one could hardly think of the one without thinking of the other. Ellis Island was the great outpost of the new and vigorous republic. [It] stood guard over the wide-flung portal. . . . Ellis Island was free of the inundating horde and largely free of carping critics, but Ellis Island has lost its proud place in the grand immigration scheme.

When Wall Street collapsed in 1929, the illusion that America was a land of gold ended abruptly. By 1932, when the Great Depression was sweeping the United States, immigrants were returning to Europe to escape America's woeful economic conditions. Those departing far outnumbered those seeking admission. In 1933, for example, 127,660 people left the United States to return home, while only about 23,000 new immigrants entered.

By World War II, Ellis Island and its service as a welcoming center and processing depot had declined almost to the vanishing point. The Coast Guard established a station on the island during the war and sailors on German or Austrian ships in the harbor were detained there when the United States government took over their country's ocean liners. Later, many aliens of German, Austrian, Italian, or Japanese origins were sent to Ellis Island for the duration. Some of them spent six or seven years on the island.

Only 1,089 immigrants were cleared through Ellis Island in 1943, 1,075 in 1944, and 2,636 in 1945. Although about 1 million immigrants entered the United States through Ellis Island between 1946 and 1954, the island was obsolete and ill-equipped, with a tired, overworked staff. It was time to bring the great story to an end.

The curtain came down on November 12, 1954, after a 62-year run. The next day, the *New York Times* provided something of an obituary:

> Without ceremony, the career of Ellis Island as an immigration center came to a virtual close yesterday. The last detained alien—a Norwegian seaman who had overstayed his shore leave—was a passenger on the Battery-

> bound ferry at 10:15 a.m. . . . The peak of immigration traffic through Ellis Island came through Ellis Island in 1907, when 1,200,000 persons were examined there. But gradually, as admission and detention procedures changed, the alien population decreased.
>
> As Attorney General Herbert Brownell explained Thursday, "The little island between the Statue of Liberty and the skyline and piers of New York seems to have served its purpose for immigration."

The island sounds of mingled voices, shuffling feet, the sobs of bitter disappointment, and the Babel of mixed tongues seemed destined to vanish into the darkness of onrushing time. No immigrants ever again would leave the ferries that had brought them to Ellis Island. No longer would thousands of newcomers move up the steps to face the examiners and the questioners in the great hall. No longer would hopeful foreigners don colorful garments in the hope of convincing examiners that they were well dressed, fit, and worthy of an American life.

Ellis Island waited, abandoned to the elements and rapidly becoming a ghost island. The millions who had begun the steps toward Americanization on Ellis now seemed of little or no importance. The inspiring yet sad and tragic stories of those mingled foreigners seeking the chance to enter a dream land began to fade into the limbo of ignorance and the dismissal of shrugged shoulders.

A few once-young immigrants now enduring old age asked a plaintive question: can America afford to let this symbol of its very soul disappear into crumbling nothingness? How long could the buildings resist the ravages of passing time, thieves, vandals, and impractical schemes?

The shrouds of hope and fear that had pervaded the island for all of its 62 years lingered on in 15 million ghosts of freedom past. The lights had been turned off.

Immigration had not stopped, but Ellis Island did not process newcomers after 1954. Few immigrants came in steerage. Most of them, largely by the circumstances of their admissions, flew into LaGuardia airport on Long Island.

A major influx of immigrants swept into the nation with great and favorable fanfare. They were the "war brides," the young foreign women that American soldiers had married abroad. A total of 120,000 of these special immigrants came to the United States soon after the war ended. All were exempt from the national quota system, although the 1920s law remained in force.

Congress finally got around to considering the plight of hundreds of thousands of homeless men, women, and children crowded together in European detention camps. Senators from rural states prolonged passage of the bill and President Truman did not sign the Displaced Persons Act until June 1948. He signed "with great reluctance" because the bill permitted only 204,000 of these desperate Europeans to enter. Truman called the bill inadequate and "flagrantly discriminatory."

After that, in large measure due to the liberalized Immigration Act of 1965, the United States offered asylum to hundreds of thousands of people between the mid-1950s and 1980. More than 30,000 Hungarians gained admission after the Russians suppressed their revolution in 1955. More than 650,000 anti-Castro Cubans came between the early 1960s and late 1970s and another 130,000 Cubans arrived in America in 1980. About 360,000 Indonesians found their way to the United States between 1975 and 1980.

Legal immigrants still arrive in great numbers, along with untold numbers of illegal immigrants who cross Canadian and Mexican borders into the United States. Regardless of the circumstances of their arrivals, they are filled with the one great belief that has driven immigrants since the beginning of recorded time—the hope that no matter how bad things might be in a new land, they will be infinitely better than life in their old villages and cities.

Chapter Fourteen

RESURRECTING A NATIONAL SHRINE

No one seemed to care about Ellis Island—not government agencies, historical societies, or nationality groups; not social-minded philanthropists, charitable foundations, or journalists. No one, public or private, hastened to buy the handsomely located property, even when 1960 rumors had it that a mere $1 million might be possible for the right buyer.

One million dollars would have been ridiculous and unacceptable; the land and buildings would have been a sensational buy at almost any price. The all-but-abandoned island was home to 35 stout buildings, mostly brick; an electric-generating powerhouse; supporting facilities; and tied up at the dock, one of the ferryboats that had for so long carried immigrants to the island or to freedom on shore. Ellis Island was "surplus property" in the midst of some of the most expensive real estate in the world.

The General Service Administration's initial asking price was $6.5 million, but freely-spread rumors said that the GSA would accept considerably less if the buyer would pledge to use the facility according to administration rules for an acceptable project.

Would-be purchasers included an orphanage for foreign children, an upscale 600-room hotel with a marina and helicopter pad, a seaman's school, a gambling casino, a Bible College, an International Cathedral for Peace Prayers, and many other proposals. All were rejected.

The low point in planning the island's future came in the winter of 1958. In January of that year, the GSA offered the property—land, buildings, utilities, everything—at a public auction. Sealed bids would be opened on February 14. Between the announcement and the opening of bids, Congressman Paul A. Fino of New York suggested that Ellis Island should become a national lottery center, to honor the "legalized gambling spirit of the American people." Fino pointed out that immigrants at the island "gambled for a new life in this land of ours."

The high bidder in the auction was New York builder Sol G. Atlas, who bid $215,000. He proposed a $55 million "Pleasure Island" replete with a resort hotel, a convention center, tennis courts, a spacious marina, and, perhaps as a sop to the history-minded, a museum. Memories of suffering and triumph would be bulldozed away, lest the wealthy admirers of Pleasure Island be offended. The GSA rejected all bids in April and set a value on the island of $6,326,000.

In September 1964, United States Senator Edmund Muskie of Maine, the son of a Polish immigrant named Marcisczweski who had entered the United States through Ellis Island in 1903, chaired Senate hearings to decide the island's fate.

The National Park Service released a detailed study in 1965 that suggested making Ellis Island a part of the Statue of Liberty National Monument. President Lyndon B. Johnson did exactly that on May 11 when he formalized the marriage of Ellis Island and Lady Liberty. Congress appropriated $6 million for the development of the rapidly deteriorating island.

Plans for the buildings sprang to the fore, all of them expensive and all of them missing the simple need to tell the agonizing story of immigration rather than sinking the past in a glitter of modern embellishments. A National Park Service plan approved in November 1968 proposed preserving the main building as a museum but demolishing all other buildings except "three relatively modern buildings temporarily for use pending completion of development."

Perhaps as a symbol of the delay and indecision, the 64-year-old ferryboat *Ellis Island* could not wait any longer. In August 1968 she slipped quietly into the mud at the bottom of the channel in front of the main building.

Congress had failed to allot money to guard properly the buildings or to secure the grounds. Withdrawal of guards encouraged thieves to plunder the area, carrying away plumbing fixtures, chandeliers, furniture, and machinery. Signs were ripped off the walls and sold in New York as mementos. The most daring heist was carried out by nimble invaders who climbed the main building to pry away the copper sheathing that capped the towers.

Despite the fact that little had been accomplished beyond a superficial cleaning, the National Park Service rangers began one-hour tours of the structure in September 1976. *New York Times* reporter Sidney H. Schanberg visited the island, apparently hoping there might be something to conjure up romantic visions of the vanished days when immigrants streamed through the building by the thousands. Instead he wrote, "Elllis Island is about as romantic as a row of hollow buildings in the South Bronx." (The South Bronx, for those who did not know it, was a drug-ridden, burned-out section of Harlem.) Schanberg gave vivid details of the main building, the only place where superficial work had been done:

> This one has been shored up and rendered safe, but it is moldering. Interior walls have crumbled. Mounds of fallen plaster and pools of rainwater from

> leaking roofs spread darkly across some of the floors. Dust and peeling paint are the most benign signs of the slow rot. Windows are out and in one room moss and small trees are growing, and pigeons have settled in. Here and there some bits of salvaged old furniture have been arranged forlornly in an attempt to recapture the era.

The once-revered, once-feared island got a new life in 1982, when the Statue of Liberty/Ellis Island Foundation was formed, headed by Lee Iacocca, internationally known and respected automobile manufacturing executive. More than 20 million people donated more than $160 million for the restoration of the northern end of Ellis Island. It would be one of the largest, if not the largest, building restoration projects ever undertaken in the United States.

Architects were instructed to restore the building in such a fashion that it could be used as a huge museum to trace and interpret the immigrant experience—not only of Ellis Island but also of all the United States and much of the rest of the world. First the building had to be stabilized and dried out. This process took about two years. Restoration centered on the huge Registration Room, the core of the sturdy structure and the place where millions upon millions of newcomers had threaded their way through the physical, mental, and character testing that would determine their fitness to enter America.

The high, vaulted ceiling was the greatest potential challenge and also the most rewarding triumph. The ceiling had been tiled in the 1920s after an explosion in 1916 at a nearby armament storage depot shattered the old ceiling. The replacement tiling was planned and set in place by the Guastavino Brothers, Italian immigrants widely known for their tile expertise. The Guastavinos worked without scaffolding, preferring to work while hanging from safety belts attached to the roof.

Restoration workers practiced no such heroics. They filled the entire reception room with scaffolding, topped by platforms that permitted workers to snuggle close to the ceiling. They tested each of the 28,282 tiles, making sure that all were still solidly in place. A few broken tiles were found, but remarkably, only 17 needed replacing.

Modern-day visitors might not even notice the ceiling, but the overall beauty of the restoration is hard to escape anywhere in the building. Restorers worked faithfully to reproduce original colors and designs. The many old steam radiators, for example, were all pressure tested and painted. Most of the old radiators easily passed the pressure test and were finished with glossy banana oil paint that was used when they were installed in the 1890s.

The huge half-circle windows that run completely around the edges of the ceiling and let in natural light were all meticulously checked and repaired where necessary. Natural light also sweeps into the room through the large windows that line walls beneath the balcony that encircles the lower part of the hall.

All of this now embellishes the reception area, first revealed to the public when the restored building was opened in 1990. Beyond is the extensive, easy to-comprehend museum that traces immigration back to America's first settlers and continues the story to the present. Rooms in the two upper floors contain theme exhibits that explore the reasons for leaving revered homelands throughout Europe in the early part of the twentieth century, then carry the story through steerage, the examination process at Ellis Island, and into the jobs they found and neighborhoods where they settled.

More than two million visitors stream through the museum doors each year. Nearly all of them stay long enough to get at least some sympathetic and appreciative awareness of the courage and determination of the Ellis Island immigrants. Visitors leave, board a ferryboat, and continue to the Statue of Liberty, where another emotional face of immigration awaits them.

Apprehensive immigrants dressed in the bright clothing of their homelands no longer stand in lines, but their descendants come and better understand the saga of their resolute forebears—and, if they wish, learn some of the new computerized methods that help them personalize their immigrant connections.

Ellis Island has a future that very few of the two million annual visitors have ever seen, or can even imagine. Ellis Island for most visitors is the main building, the focal point for all but a tiny portion of tourists. It was built on the original island, now grown to about three times its original size thanks to massive infusions of fill in the first decade of the twentieth century. To the south of the ferry slip, where incoming ferries tie up, is the rest of Ellis Island, about 15-plus acres. This is also all "new " land created in the 1890s and early twentieth century to provide undergirding for new and vital supporting facilities for the reception center.

It is not that the enlargement of the island (to seven or eight times the original size) is a secret. As the ferryboats dock, anyone can look south and see major buildings lined up on the opposite side of the channel. Those are hospital structures, and behind them are more than a dozen contagious disease and quarantine buildings, all built between 1902 and 1908, at the time of the greatest arrival of newcomers from Europe.

This almost-forgotten portion of Ellis Island has been stabilized since 1990. A second-growth forest has been cut away, sidewalks are attractive, and lawns are well maintained, but that is as far as it goes. When money was being raised for reclaiming the island, there was talk and written policy that indicated all, or at least most, of the buildings would be restored. Nearly all of the millions of dollars and funds went to restore the main hall and its grounds. It was judged adequate merely to maintain the southern part of the island. It became a secured but little changed ghost town.

President Franklin D. Roosevelt, a liberal Democrat, joined the forces that wanted restricted immigration. His concern was almost totally based on economic reality: any tide of immigrants to America would dangerously diminish the jobs for the millions of unemployed men and women caught in the web of an increasing major depression.

In a stroke of irony, much of that neglected portion of Ellis Island was built up in the 1930s, more than two decades after the huge crowds of immigrants had flowed into and out of the main building. By 1930, immigration had slowed to a trickle. The U.S. government turned to federal agencies such as the Works Progress Administration and offered jobs to many builders and craftsmen.

In an even greater stroke of irony, the Roosevelt administration put those now federally employed Americans to work erecting a spate of buildings on the southern portion of the island, along with a new ferry house and an area where immigrants could wait for ferries. The government-paid workers also filled in the wide channel that once had split the southern portion of the island.

None of that mattered much when the island was closed in 1954. As funds began to be available through the Statue of Liberty/Ellis Island Foundation, the National Park Service conducted a competition for ideas on ways to use the southern portion of the island. William Hubbard, president of the nonprofit Center for Housing Partnerships, won with a plan that captured none of the reality of Ellis Island as a haven for the tired, the poor, or the hungry masses yearning to breathe free.

Hubbard's plan called for restoring and adaptively using more than 30 buildings as a hotel and conference center.. While the National Park Service was generally supportive, it had to be discomfited by Hubbard's vision of tennis courts, swimming pools, a health center, and a marina. If any one of the millions of immigrants had been asked to define such words, it is unlikely they would have scored 100 percent.

In September 1986, the Hubbard plan, stripped of its posh amenities, was changed into an international conference center managed by area universities, a place said to be in the exquisite nicety of Versailles or Geneva. That also died a dignified but little mourned death.

In 1998, the U.S. Supreme Court awarded New Jersey sovereignty over 22 acres of Ellis Island, including that southern portion where restoration was a mockery of the word. In contrast, the remaining 5.5 acres, including the restored and highly envied main building, was given to New York. It was another of the strange rulings on the island that have favored New York ever since the quarrel over jurisdiction rose as early as 1834.

There matters stood until the summer of 2003, when the National Park Service resuscitated hopes for developing the south side of the island. The plans called for $300 million in federal and private funds to complete the job of bringing Ellis fully back to life. Public hearings were held in New York and New Jersey to gauge the reaction on such things as an ethnic diversity institute, a public health museum, and a self sustaining hotel-conference center, not likely, at least in the beginning years, to have a swimming pool or marina.

Cynthia Garret, acting superintendent of the Statue of Liberty Monument and Ellis Island, called the proffered plan "our last, best chance for preservation." Park officials and a New Jersey preservation group, Save Ellis Island, hoped to raise $300 million to revive the south part of Ellis.

Save Ellis Island leaders believed it would take five years to raise the money necessary to save the 30 structures seriously damaged by years of neglect, salt air, and vandalism. That would make 2008 the year before work could begin.

New Jersey can wait. New Jersey must wait and so must the world.

IMMIGRANTS OF CONSEQUENCE

Although every immigrant who passed through Ellis Island and Castle Garden contributed in some way to the collective culture and life of a growing United States, hundreds of them achieved fame and, in some cases, fortunes as American citizens. This is a representative listing of a few very well-known immigrants who succeeded in a variety of careers. Their lives serve to show that for some at least, the dream could become reality.

Isaac Asimov, one of America's leading authors of science fiction, was born in Russia and entered the United States in 1923, at age 3.

Irving Berlin entered through Ellis Island from Russia in 1892 at age 4 and became America's most prolific and beloved songwriter. His hundreds of popular tunes include "White Christmas" and "God Bless America."

Frank Capra, often hailed as Hollywood's foremost director in the 1930s and 1940s, came to the United States from Italy in 1903 at age 6.

David Dubinsky, named David Qobniewaki when he came from Poland in 1910 as a 19-year-old, was the first member of the International Ladies Garment Workers Union. He became the union president and was an adviser to President Franklin D. Roosevelt.

Edward Flanagan, who came through Ellis Island from Ireland in August 1904 at age 18, became a priest, and in 1917 founded the project for which he became world-famous: Boys Town.

Felix Frankfurter, son of a Viennese merchant, came with his family in 1894. He graduated from City College of New York and from Harvard Law School. He was appointed to the United States Supreme Court in 1939.

Emma Goldman, said to be "the most interesting radical ever to pass through Ellis Island," entered from Russia in 1886 at age 17 via Castle Garden. After a tumultuous career in the United States as an anarchist, she was deported from Ellis Island on December 21, 1919 during the so-called "Red Scare."

Samuel Goldwyn entered in 1894 at age 11 under his real name Samuel Foldfish. He took the last name Goldwyn when he became a naturalized citizen in 1902 and as Samuel Goldwyn achieved fame as one of America's best known film producers.

Samuel Gompers, born in London of Dutch-Jewish parents, began cigar making at age 10 and in 1863 entered America through Castle Garden. He rose through the ranks and served as president of the American Federation of Labor for 40 years.

Bob Hope, who entered the United States in 1908 at age 5, became a famous comedian, starring in radio shows, films, and television, and earned distinction for entertaining American troops during World War II.

Al Jolson, born in Lithuania, came to the United States in 1894 at age 8. He became a star in vaudeville, then in motion pictures and radio as an actor and a singer.

Golda Meir arrived in Milwaukee via Ellis Island in 1908, after fleeing Russia with her family. She left America to go to Palestine in 1921, was a strong factor in the creation of Israel in 1948, and served as prime minister of the new state from 1969 to 1984.

Philip Murray, a 16-year-old from Wales, arrived at Ellis Island in 1902. He became a leading member of the United Steelworkers of America and the C.I.O.

Jacob Riis, a Danish immigrant, passed through Castle Garden in 1870 and became a leading American social reformer.

Hyman G. Rickover, one of the great admirals of the United States Navy in World War II, was born in Poland in 1898 and came to the United States in 1904 at age 6.

Edward G. Robinson, born in Romania in 1893, entered the United States through Ellis Island in 1903 at age 10, and won fame as a motion picture actor, particularly as a smooth-talking gangster boss.

Knute Rockne, one of the nation's greatest football coaches in a long career at Notre Dame University, came from Norway to the United States in 1893 as a 5-year-old boy. He graduated from Notre Dame and was a chemistry instructor before becoming the football coach at his alma mater.

Karl Auguste Rudolf Steinmetz, a highly educated German scientist, fled his homeland and arrived in steerage in 1889 and was cleared through Castle Garden. Woefully crippled, he became a noted engineer at General Electric Company, and in time was known as "the wizard of G.E."

Rudolph Valentino, who entered as a youth from Italy in 1913, started his career as a bit part dancer. Eight years later he was the reigning idol of the silent screen era, appearing in such films as *Blood and Sand* and *The Shiek*.

BIBLIOGRAPHY

Archdeacon, Thomas J. *Becoming American, An Ethnic History.* New York: The Free Press, 1983.

Brownstone, David M., Irene M. Franck, and Douglass L. Brownstone. *Island of Hope, Island of Tears.* New York: Rawson, Wade Publishers, 1979.

Coan, Peter Morton. *Ellis Island Interviews.* New York: Checkmark Books, 1997.

Dunne, Thomas, and Wilson Tift. *Ellis Island.* New York: W.W. Norton, 1971.

Eaton, John P., and Charles A. Haas. *Titanic, Triumph and Tragedy.* New York: W.W. Norton, 1986.

Gallo, Patrick. *Old Bread, New Wine.* Chicago: Nelson-Hall, Inc., 1981.

Maisel, Albert Q. *They All Chose America.* New York: Thomas Nelson & Sons, 1955.

Marcus, Geoffrey. *The Maiden Voyage, The Titanic Epic.* New York: The Viking Press, 1969.

Morison, Samuel Eliot. *The Oxford History of the American People.* New York: Oxford University Press, 1965.

Morrison, Joan, and Charlotte Fox Zabusky. *American Mosaic.* Pittsburgh: University of Pittsburgh Press, 1993.

Novotny, Ann. *Stranger at the Door.* New York: Bantam Pathfinder Editions, 1974.

Parillo, Vincent N. *Strangers to These Shores.* New York: Allyn and Bacon, 1985.

Pitkin, Thomas M.N. *Keepers of the Gate, a History of Ellis Island.* New York: New York University Press, 1975.

Reeves, Pamela. *Ellis Island, Gateway to the American Dream.* New York: Crescent Books, 2000.

Seller, Maxine Schwartz. *Immigrant Women.* Philadelphia: Temple University Press, 1981.

Steiner, Edward A. *On the Trail of the Immigrant.* New York: Fleming H. Revell Co., 1906.

Taylor, Philip. *The Distant Magnet, European Emigration to the United States.* New York: Harper & Rowe, 1971.

Tift, Wilson S. *Ellis Island.* Chicago: Contemporary Books, 1990.

Wilson, Woodrow. *A History of the American People.* New York: Harper and Brothers, 1902.

Yans-McLaughlin, Virginia, and Marjorie Lightman. *Ellis Island and the Peopling of America (The Official Guide).* New York: The Free Press, 1995.

INDEX

Abuse of immigrants, 29, 38, 39, 98–100, 106, 125, 128, 129, 132
Admission tests, 61, 116, 118, 121–125, 127, 130, 141, 142, 149
Aid to immigrants, 105, 123, 126, 130, 131
Ancestors, immigrant, 11, 20, 28, 138, 150
Archdeacon, Thomas J., 131, 132
Asian Americans, 33, 38, 144
Baggage, 35, 39, 61, 99, 115, 120, 133, 134
Baltimore, Lord, 15, 16
Barge Office, 59–61, 63, 99
Barnum, Phineas T., 30
Barth, Helen, 123
Bartholdi, Frederic Auguste, 41–46, 56
Battery, The, 29, 30, 31, 4, 56, 58, 59, 62, 134, 145
Bedloe's Island, 40–42, 44, 46, 56, 57
Board of Special Inquiry, 130
Bundles and suitcases, 104, 106, 143
Burials at sea, 33, 107, 109
California, 13, 37, 52
Canals, 24, 25, 27, 51
Cartoons, immigrant, 50
Castle Garden
  early history, 29–31
  immigration center, 29, 31–40, 41, 54, 59, 97, 99, 101
  Labor Exchange, 35
  abandonment, 40
Catholics, 15, 20, 22, 24–26, 50, 135–138, 140
Celluloid, 48
"Chalking", 121, 122
Civil Service, 99
Class, First or Second, 34, 105, 107, 110, 111, 113, 114–117, 130, 133
Cleveland, President Grover, 38, 46
Coal mines, 25, 35, 37, 48, 51, 135, 136, 140
"coffin ships", 23
Colonial immigration, 13–18, 20
Columbus, Christopher, 13
Commerce and Labor Department, U.S., 107, 130
Commissioners, Immigration, 28, 31, 32, 36, 38–40, 60, 62, 97–99, 119, 124–126, 128, 129, 131, 142, 144
Communists, 142
Corruption, 38, 97–99
Corsi, Edward, 126, 130, 131
Curran, Harry, 131, 143
Currency exchange, 35, 36, 61, 97–99, 120, 125
Declaration of Independence, 20, 28, 42
Deportation
  Reasons, 33, 122, 125, 127–131, 142
  Appeals, 130
Diseases, 22, 23, 25, 26, 28, 29, 32, 59, 63, 64, 101, 107, 113, 122
Disease susceptibility, 23, 25, 26, 32, 113
Duke of York, 17
Dutch West India Company, 15
Ellis Island
  admission process, 24, 31, 59, 60, 97, 98, 105, 118–127, 131, 142, 144, 145
  early history, 40, 41, 57–60
  closing, 144–146
  construction, first building, 58, 59
  construction, second building, 63, 64
  fire, 62
  modern museum, 148–150
Embarkation ports, 29, 33, 102, 103, 105, 109, 123, 128
Employment, 24, 27, 35, 49–51, 53, 54, 99, 117, 118, 126, 129, 133–137, 150, 151
Exhibit areas, 150
Explorers, 12–16

Factories, 21, 24, 25, 48, 49, 51, 53, 54, 100, 134–136, 139
Famous Ellis Island immigrants, 153–155
Fires at sea, 33
Ferries, 34, 46, 58, 61, 63, 117, 118, 134, 145, 147, 148, 150, 151
Food, steerage, 19, 22, 32, 53, 107, 108
Food, immigration depots, 97, 98
Fort Wood, 41
France, 13, 41–46, 51, 105
Funds from America, 55, 102, 103, 105, 132, 139
General Service Administration, 147, 148
Germans, 17, 20, 21, 27, 28, 33, 34, 36, 59, 62, 105, 108, 110, 119, 124, 137–139, 141, 144, 155
Governor's Island, 30, 40, 56
Herring, 54, 57, 108, 114, 115
Half Moon, 14
Holland, 14, 15, 105
Howe, Frederick, 141, 142
Hudson, Henry, 13, 14
Hudson River, 13, 14, 16, 23, 27, 34, 59, 115–117, 133
Indies, the, 12, 13, 28
Indians ("Original People")
  Tribal names, 12, 15
  Areas of settlement, 12, 18, 57
  Tribal culture, 12, 15
Industry, 24, 25, 37, 38, 48, 50, 51, 117, 135
Interpreters, 123, 125, 142
Iacocca. Lee, 149
Irish, 15, 20–28, 34, 36, 39, 60–62, 102, 103, 105, 108, 111, 119, 136–139, 143, 153
Iron mines, 35, 48, 51, 59, 135
Island of Hope, Island of Tears, 104, 108, 109, 114, 115, 117
Jamestown, 14, 15
Jews, 47, 53, 101, 106, 124, 135, 138, 154
"Kissing Post", 126
"Know Nothings", 26
Johnson, President Lyndon B., 148
Labor,
  child, 100, 136, 138, 139
  contract, 38, 124
  organized, 38, 50, 59, 97, 136, 138
Landing docks, 23–25, 28–30, 34, 36, 58, 63, 116–119, 133, 147
Languages, 12, 17, 34, 119, 120, 123, 125, 140, 141
Laws, immigrant, 23, 32, 37, 38, 57, 59, 99, 100, 105, 124, 128, 131, 136, 141, 143–145
Lazarus, Emma, 12, 22, 47
Letters from America, 22, 23, 35, 54, 103, 124, 128
Lind, Jenny, 30
Manhattan, 12, 14, 15, 17, 116
Manifests, 12, 32, 33, 59, 60
Marriages on Ellis Island, 125, 126
Maryland, 15, 16, 20
Martucci, Frank, 125, 126
Mayflower, 11, 16, 17
Money, 22, 27, 32, 35–37, 39, 42, 44, 45, 55, 60, 61, 97–99, 102–105, 111, 113, 115, 117, 118, 120, 124–126, 128, 130–133, 137, 138, 142, 148, 151, 152
Morison, Samuel Eliot, 11, 18
Muskie, Senator Edmund, 148
Name changes, 123, 124, 153, 154
National Park Service, 148, 151, 152
Need for immigrants, 19–21, 24, 25, 37, 49–53, 135
"new immigrants", 53, 139, 140
New Amsterdam, 15, 17, 57
New Jersey, 12, 14, 16, 17, 19, 25, 27, 33, 35, 37, 40, 41, 45, 48, 51, 57, 58, 62, 116, 129, 133–135, 137, 138, 151, 152
New Sweden, 15, 17
New York City, 25, 27–31, 35, 36, 40, 45, 48, 51, 56–58, 60–62, 116, 120, 129, 133, 134, 136
New York Times, 32, 42, 43, 45, 46, 60, 61, 142, 144, 148
New York World, 38, 39, 45, 56
Newspaper articles, 26, 38, 39, 42, 43, 45, 50, 56, 60, 61, 99, 124, 148, 149
Novotny, Ann, 114, 134, 138
Opponents of immigration, 124, 138, 141
Oyster Islands, 41, 57
Parillo, Vincent, 49
Paris, 41, 42, 44, 45, 47, 56
Philadelphia Centennial Exposition, 42
Plymouth, 16, 17

Index

Pogroms, Russian, 47, 101, 106, 109, 119
Politics, 24, 26, 27, 38, 39, 49, 97–99, 119, 130
Potato famine, 21, 22, 24, 25
Propaganda to emigrate, 19, 20, 49–54, 101–103
Proprietors, royal, 18–20, 25
Pulitzer, Joseph, 28, 39, 45, 56
Puritans, 16, 20
Quarantine, 34, 62, 63, 98116, 150
Quakers, 17, 20
Queenstown, Ireland, 102
Railroads, 24, 25, 27, 31, 35–39, 41, 46, 48, 49, 51–53, 56, 61, 63, 97, 98, 100, 103, 120, 124, 125, 133–137
Railroad land, 49, 52, 53
"Red Scare", 142, 154
Registry Hall, 64, 98, 120, 123, 129, 145, 150, 151
Religion, 12, 16, 18, 20, 27
Roanoke Island, 14
Roosevelt, President Theodore, 97–99, 124
Sailing vessels, 13–17, 22, 27, 28, 32, 34, 37, 41, 108–110, 112, 113
Scandinavians, 13, 15, 17, 20, 34, 54, 62, 103, 110, 111, 119, 144, 154, 155
Seamen, German and Austrian, 141, 144
Sewing machines, 48, 134, 136
Siberia, 11, 12
Slaves, 19, 21
Smith, Captain John, 16
Spain, 13, 15
Statue of Liberty
  collecting for the statue, 43–45
  completion in New York, 46
  copper plates, 42–46
  dedication, 41, 46, 47
  iron "skeleton", 44–46
  shipment to America, 45, 46
Statue of Liberty National Monument, 148, 152
Steamships, 52, 53, 60, 61, 105, 110–114, 117, 118, 130, 142
Steamship companies, 49, 51, 53, 59, 62, 99, 105, 108, 110, 111, 114, 124, 128, 130, 133
Steiner, Edward, 97, 98, 112, 122
Steerage, 22, 23, 27, 29, 32–34, 51, 53, 58–61, 64, 97–99, 105–116, 119, 122, 123, 125, 128, 130, 134, 138, 142, 145, 150, 155
"surplus property", 147
Tenements, 137, 138
Textiles, 37, 48, 136, 138
The Distant Magnet, 54, 112
Thieves and swindlers, 22, 29, 36, 38, 63, 97, 98, 104, 138, 148
Titanic, 110, 111
Trachoma, 108, 121, 122, 128, 130
Traditions, 101, 102, 139
Treasury Department, U.S., 39, 56, 57, 59, 107
Vespucci, Amerigo, 13
Vessels, colonial, 13–17, 22
Wallis, Frederick, 128, 129
Washington, President George, 21, 26, 39
Watchorn, Robert, 99, 100, 119, 125
Welfare agencies, 35, 100
Western lands, 24, 27, 28, 37, 49, 52, 135
Williams, William, 98–100, 124, 125
Wilson, Woodrow, 50, 141, 142
Windom, William, 56–58, 60
Women, single, 103, 113, 126, 129
World War I, 140, 141
World War II, 140, 143, 144, 154